The Saturday Morning Gardener

A Guide to Once-a-Week Maintenance

Revised Edition

Donald Wyman

COLLIER BOOKS

A Division of Macmillan Publishing Co., Inc.
NEW YORK

COLLIER MACMILLAN PUBLISHERS
LONDON

Macmillan Publishing Co., Inc.
866 Third Avenue, New York, N. Y. 10022
Collier-Macmillan Canada Ltd.

Library of Congress Cataloging in Publication Data

Wyman, Donald, 1903–
     The Saturday morning gardener.

     1. Gardening.   I. Title.
SB453.W9   1974   635.9   73-11833
ISBN 0-02-632100-9
ISBN 0-02-063950-3 (pbk.)

The Saturday Morning Gardener is also published in a hard-
cover edition by Macmillan Publishing Co., Inc.

Revised Edition

First Collier Books Edition 1974
Second Printing 1974
Printed in the United States of America

Preface

The objective in this book is to point out to the busy gardener the many shortcuts he can take to make a beautiful garden with a minimum amount of effort. The book is divided into four main parts: Planning a Garden; Shortcuts and Aids in Maintenance; Low Maintenance Plant Lists; A–Z Listing of Low Maintenance Plants.

Proper planning saves costly errors later. Shortcuts and aids in maintenance reduce garden effort and expense. Most important of all is the proper selection of low maintenance plants—just the right ones for just the right place. There are over 900 in the following pages from which to choose.

The lists of low maintenance plants (see Chapters 3 and 4) include only those plants which we found to be generally insect- and disease-free. All others have been excluded. The low maintenance garden is not the place for plants which are known in advance to require special attention. The gardener with plenty of time can experiment to his heart's content, but some of us simply do not have that kind of time and want to reduce our garden work to a minimum. This book offers succinct information for doing just that. It should be used as a guide to once-a-week maintenance.

The lists of low maintenance plants for special purposes are designed to give pertinent information at a glance—the name of the plant, height, hardiness zone, and in some cases, color of flower, time of flower, and color of fruit; whether it is an evergreen, a tree, a shrub or perennial. If one wants a ground cover, merely turn to pages 127–133 and there they are. If one's garden has a shady spot, pages 158–166 list all low maintenance plants withstanding shade conditions. If one wants to find a little more information about these plants, the alphabetical descriptions (pages 197–359) will give it, but, for those in a hurry, most pertinent facts will be in the lists.

For more detailed information the gardener can consult *Wyman's Gardening Encyclopedia,* published by Macmillan Publishing Co., Inc., but the most important facts needed to make plant selections quickly will all be easily found in the following pages.

Acknowledgments

I am most indebted to my wife Florence Dorward Wyman, who not only read and reread the original manuscript and typed it several times but who also grew most of the bulbs, perennials, and smaller shrubs in her low maintenance garden, keeping notes on their performance through the years. The information on "dual purpose" plants was a result of her efforts and interest over a long period. Thanks are also due my daughter, Barbara Wyman Skiff, who typed the manuscript for this revised edition.

Constance B. Schrader, Senior Editor at Macmillan Publishing Co., Inc., made many excellent suggestions for the revised manuscript, all of which have been gratefully accepted and worked into the text.

Robert G. Williams, Superintendent of the Arnold Arboretum, made the excellent drawings. Grateful thanks should also be given to the staff members of the Arnold

Arboretum, who through the years have materially aided us in our knowledge of these plants, most of which have been grown in the Arnold Arboretum in Boston, Massachusetts.

Contents

Introduction

The "simple art" of caring for one's garden today
has become a baffling and complex task, requiring a
knowledge of pests, "controls," the many new varieties
of plants, and their many special requirements. Com-
pare the simplicity of gardening in early colonial times,
when the homeowner was not bothered with a multi-
tude of insects and diseases. His lawn was a patch of
grass to be hand-scythed occasionally, or left as pas-
ture for his cows, goats, or sheep. He kept the plants
that were there, or he dug some from the woods nearby.
Only as life brought more leisure, did the colonists
begin to landscape their grounds, enlarge their gardens, and gradually bring in rare plants from the woods
and import others from abroad.

Since those early times, literally hundreds of destructive insects and diseases have appeared. At the
same time, many plants that require constant attention

have gained acceptance because they are unusual—or just plain cantankerous, a challenge to the gardener's skill just to keep them alive. With the gradual accumulation of this kind of plant and the dramatic increase in insect pests and diseases, garden chores have increased tremendously, for they must be performed regularly if the plants are to be kept in good condition.

All this means that supplying garden accessories is truly big business today. The home gardener can ride in comfort as he cuts his lawn, fertilize it at the same time that he turns on his hose, and aerate the soil by punching holes in it with a mechanized roller. If weeds appear, there is a plethora of chemicals to kill them; if soils dry out too quickly, there are a dozen different mulches available. All too often, the homeowner invests in far more equipment and material than is necessary.

Which brings me to the point that there are two kinds of gardener. One is willing to spend large amounts of time and money to have beautiful plantings. He thinks nothing of hiring gardeners or spending a large proportion of his own spare time to see that pruning, weeding, grass cutting, and spraying are all done perfectly and on time, with the best of materials and equipment.

The second kind includes those who admire a pleasant garden, but through lack of time, money, physical strength, or because of the competition of other interests or responsibilities, cannot allow gardening to absorb too much of their spare time and money. It is to this group of gardeners that this book is primarily addressed—those who are continually on the lookout for new labor-saving devices, truly low maintenance plants, and the many shortcuts that will make garden upkeep easier.

There is a strong case to be made today for planting the smaller shrubs and the smaller trees—in terms of lower cost and reduced maintenance. Many of the new houses being built nowadays are only about fifteen to twenty-five feet high. Tall-growing shrubs—like the Common Lilac—that can reach the third story of an old-fashioned house, if used near a small home, will need constant pruning to be kept to a proportioned height. Not only that, but the Common Lilac, if allowed to go unpruned, can grow as wide as it is tall—twenty feet at least—sending out lateral suckers that must be restrained by pruning almost every year. If the modern homeowner must have a lilac and no other shrub will do, plant a lilac by all means, but make a mental commitment at planting time to prune the shrub regularly to keep it within proper bounds. For the person who is willing to take a substitute for the lilac, there are many other plants that will mature at lower heights and will not need repeated pruning to be kept in scale.

In the same way, planting smaller trees may be far more practical today. At one time a home planting was not complete without a stately elm overshadowing the house. Elms grow over a hundred feet high, and in recent years many a property owner has found to his sorrow what it costs to remove one of these giants once it becomes diseased and starts to die. Smaller trees— trees that grow only twenty-five or thirty-five feet tall— are frequently just as serviceable and attractive. They will give beauty and shade, they will grow above the roof of the small house, and still not be so costly to remove if it should become necessary to do so. Nor will they be so expensive to prune and spray.

Ground covers are another important asset for the low maintenance garden. Their extensive use can provide a weed-free and attractive underplanting for shrubs and trees.

In summary, smaller shrubs, lower trees, and

ground covers are the all-important low maintenance plants to be used about the small home grounds. Not all are easily found in every nursery catalogue for many nurserymen have not yet recognized the demand for some of these plants. But all are being grown somewhere in this country, and most are available. If local nurseries fail to provide some of these plants, sources can be recommended by state agricultural colleges, horticultural societies, and the various arboretums and botanical gardens.

1
___

Planning a Garden

Every garden should be beautiful as well as utilitarian. The smaller the area, the more important it is to make a careful choice. Keep in mind always *how long* each plant has beauty and interest. The shrub or tree that is attractive for only a week or two while in bloom, but which has no good autumn color or interesting fruits, should be discarded. Choose instead ones that have outstanding flowers in the spring, good form all year round, bright-colored fruits in summer, and a vivid autumn beauty. There are such plants and they deserve prime consideration in any garden plan. If they can be chosen from among those plants that require minimum care, you can establish a garden that is both beautiful and easy to care for.

The most important way to save labor later on is to plan the garden intelligently from the first. The first thing to do, then, is to make an overall plan. If you start with a completely empty space, you are free to create your garden from scratch. If you inherit a garden which already has plantings, make an inventory of them and keep only the ones that you like. Be ruthless about discarding those that do not fit in with your final design.

Whether you start with an empty garden, or with existing trees and shrubs, once the house is in place and the drives and walks have been located, a number of other factors will influence your choice of plantings and where you will need to put them.

PERSONAL NEEDS

In the first place, how is the garden to be used? For entertaining, some area should be set aside near the house—preferably a terrace or patio—suitably shielded by evergreens and hedges to insure year-round privacy. For smaller homes, the "outdoor living room" is often merely a small patio, or a corner of the house where shade, and possibly a pool or fountain, help provide a peaceful, relaxing atmosphere. Modern homes tend to be discarding the old-fashioned, built-in outdoor fireplaces; the small, portable charcoal grills make fire building and cooking far simpler.

For the larger gardens, space may be needed for a game area: a badminton court (44' x 20'), a tennis court (78' x 36'), a basketball backboard, or space for some other game requires careful planning. If a swimming pool is going to be installed, its location should be decided on even before the trees are placed, since the source of water supply and drainage are essential factors in its location. If there are small children in a family, their needs should certainly be considered. A secluded area, near enough to the house to be able to check on easily, in shade, and where possibly a sandbox could be located, would be a very desirable asset.

Two service areas may be needed: a laundry yard, suitably hidden by a fence or hedge, or some arrangement for a collapsible laundry wheel or permanent hooks for connecting lines; and an area for a dog run, again suitably screened and fenced, or some arrangement for an exercise line included.

Will you plan to have a vegetable garden, and how large will it be? When we moved into a new house while our children were still very young, we wanted a vegetable garden, but planned it so that it was large enough to be made into a tennis court when our children were older.

Do you plan to grow annuals, perennials, and bulbs in large quantities, or are there to be just a few here and there around the foundation planting. Will you plan to have regular flower borders—if so, they should be planned to take advantage of full sun, away from trees whose roots compete for water and nourishment.

These are all personal needs that should be thought out and carefully planned before deciding on your final garden design, a design that should include provision for future needs as well as current ones.

TREES

Once recreational and service needs have been decided on, placing the trees should be next on the agenda. First, decide what the trees are to contribute to the planting scheme. Some will certainly be chosen to shade certain parts of the house or terrace or play area. If it's shade that's needed, where is it to fall, and how tall and how wide must a tree or trees be to give the proper amount of shade on the proper place at the

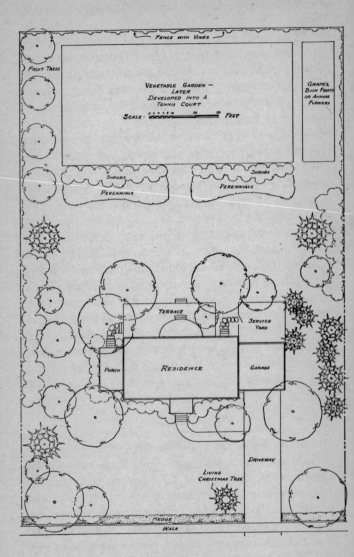

Inside the plan the following labels appear:

FENCE WITH VINES

FRUIT TREES

VEGETABLE GARDEN —
LATER
DEVELOPED INTO A
TENNIS COURT

SCALE: 0 2 4 6 10 20 30 FEET

GRAPES, BUSH FRUITS OR ANNUAL FLOWERS

SHRUBS

PERENNIALS

SHRUBS

PERENNIALS

TERRACE

SERVICE YARD

PORCH

RESIDENCE

GARAGE

DRIVEWAY

LIVING CHRISTMAS TREE

HEDGE

WALK

A good garden plan.

proper time? This is important to plan for, for once a tree is well on its way to mature growth, it is both expensive and difficult to move.

Trees are also used to give an interesting background to a house when viewed from the main road, or even to frame the house, as in a picture.

To some people, such considerations may be more important even than providing shade to parts of the house or garden. Again, some trees are used to screen off objectionable views, and still others are chosen merely for beauty of flower, fruit, or autumn color. It is extremely important, in the new planting, that tree placement be given very careful consideration, for trees should be planted as soon as possible, and much thought should go into the selection of just the right species for the right places.

The expected spread of the tree branches is another important factor in placing trees properly. Small trees, for instance, like the crab apples, dogwoods, Japanese Maples and magnolias will eventually have a spread of 20 feet. Medium-sized trees like the Canoe Birch, Katsura-tree, lindens, and Sorrel-tree may have a spread of 30 to 35 feet. Large trees like the beech, Ginkgo, Sweet-gum, Honey-locust, maples, cedars, pines, hemlocks, etc., may have spreads of 40 feet or more. When planning where to place a tree near a house, these factors must be kept in mind. The branches of a tree planted too near the house may eventually touch it or rub it and have to be removed, spoiling the shape of the tree.

One other point might be kept in mind which can save on early maintenance. Usually a tree 7 to 8 feet tall at planting time will grow faster the first few years than a 12 to 14 foot tree. Additional money can be spent on providing the small tree with the best possible soil and growth conditions, so that sometimes it may pay to buy smaller trees at the start. If, however, large trees must be moved in to give immediate shade or beauty, one must be prepared for additional expense and maintenance in providing perfect growing conditions for these larger trees to grow quickly and normally. It can be done.

Trees are also used for their conspicuous flowers (dogwoods, magnolias, and crab apples) and for their beauty of form and habits of growth. The Flowering Dogwood and many conifers have a horizontal branching habit; some of the maples and fastigiate English Oak are columnar in habit; while one of the European beeches is pendulous in habit. There are trees for utilitarian purposes as well as for beauty of flower, form, and foliage, and one should decide in advance just why a tree is wanted, where the best spot for it is, and what tree will serve the desired purpose best.

Finally, before planting trees, one should make certain they are not placed where their roots will feed ravenously in flower gardens. Elms, beeches, and maples are notorious for having hundreds of feeding roots very close to the surface of the soil. It is usually impossible for shrubs or flowers to grow underneath them, especially if their branches sweep the ground. To remove the lower branches of such trees, thus allowing light to reach the ground in an attempt to grow other plants underneath them, really defeats the purpose for which they were planted in the first place. Nor should they be placed near water pipes, drain pipes, or cesspools where their roots might eventually enter such pipes and clog them, causing serious maintenance problems later.

Hence, in planning the garden thought should be given to placing the trees where they best will serve their functions in the landscape plan, but will not compete for water and soil nourishment with other desired plantings or clog water and drain pipes.

THE LIVING CHRISTMAS TREE

Those who like to string colored lights on a tree at Christmas will want to choose a special spot in their garden for a living Christmas tree. Placing a specimen evergreen somewhere near the front of the house is always a good idea; it acts as a screen every day of the year and its beauty and symmetry of outline add materially to any well-planned landscape planting.

The ideal Christmas tree is a narrow-leaved evergreen that is pyramidal in habit, with stiff branches borne in whorls and with spaces between the whorls so that lights can be hung and properly displayed near the trunk of the tree as well as at the tips of the branches. Some trees, like the stiff-growing firs and spruces, are excellent as Christmas trees—their sturdy branches can be heavily strung with wires and lights without noticeable bending. Other types, like the graceful hemlocks and the White Pine, have branches that are too easily bent to display lights to good advantage. A dense-growing tree like an arborvitae is not a desirable one on which to string lights, for when the job is done, they are all on the outside of the plant. The same is true of some of the pines like the Red and Yellow Pines whose branches grow too coarsely to permit lights to be hung near the central trunk.

It might be pointed out here that certain types of trees which are popular as *cut* Christmas trees in different parts of the country (Balsam Fir in the East, Douglas-fir on the northwest Pacific Coast, White Fir in the Rocky Mountain area, and so on) may not be suitable for planting in your garden. This is particularly true of the Balsam Fir; this tree, native over a wide area in the mountainous, cooler, and more humid parts of the northern United States, does not grow well under any other conditions. It is popular as a cut tree at Christmas because it is available and inexpensive, but it should practically never be chosen for ornamental planting outside its native habitat.

The tree species that might be selected for planting (near the house and not too far from an electrical outlet) for Christmas-tree purposes are the following:

Abies species	Firs
Cedrus species	Cedars
Juniperus scopulorum	Western Red-cedar
Juniperus virginiana	Red-cedar
Libocedrus decurrens	California Incense-cedar
Picea species	Spruces
Pseudotsuga menziesii	Douglas-fir

THE DWARF-SHRUB PERENNIAL GARDEN

One of the most fascinating activities in growing plants is to experiment with new types or to place old, recognized species in new environments to see how they prosper. Without this activity, many plant growers would lose interest entirely. This section, then, is not for the young and enthusiastic gardener who wants to try anything and everything for himself. This is, of course, the best way to learn the facts of gardening, and most of us go through this stage. It takes time, money, and labor, and brings many disappointments, but it also brings interest and knowledge. The things that one learns this way seem so new and important that one tends to believe it is the first time such discoveries have been made. More power to those who approach gardening with this attitude!

There are gardeners, however, who have gone beyond this stage. They still want to plant, and they have discovered many interesting facts about growing plants, but they are anxious now to learn shortcuts so that they will still have a colorful garden in continuous bloom, but without so much hard work. It is for such gardeners that the following notes may prove of value.

My wife and I found, for instance, that some specific pests for certain plants were so predominant in our garden, or under our soil conditions, or in our area that we continually lost the plants. Take delphiniums, for instance; we tried to grow many beautiful hybrids, but with only mediocre success. Eventually, they were broken off by summer windstorms or by the root borer that seems to be vicious under our local conditions. As a result, we have resigned ourselves to the situation and do not plant delphiniums anymore.

We used to take great delight in growing new Sweet Williams from seed each year so that the following year we would have blooming plants. It paid off while we did the work, but with increasing demands on our time we had to eliminate them also.

Then there were the annuals: there is nothing so good for summer color as annuals, and years ago we planted large numbers of these every spring. It was fun to grow them, first germinating them in tin cans, after having sterilized the soil in the pressure cooker. Then we planted them in flats and grew them in the electric hotbed, which incidentally is an extremely important garden asset. In later years we merely sowed the seed and let someone else take care of the seedlings in a greenhouse, but we did the actual planting in the garden.

At first weeds were a necessary adjunct of growing annuals, and we welcomed the time we spent battling them in the fresh air of spring and summer. But one year we left the garden unattended for six weeks, and on our return, could hardly find the annuals for the weeds. After that, and with other more important things demanding our attention, garden weeding had so many drawbacks that we began to reduce the number of annuals. We planted more of the tried and true perennials, merely to take up space in the garden, since we did not want to turn the land back into lawn. However, we did not give up the annuals altogether, but relegated them to a cutting garden by themselves, where they were planted in rows and cultivated by machine—a much easier method of raising annuals, at least for us.

This left the garden uninteresting in summer, and especially so in the fall and winter. It was then that we started to plant a few dwarf shrubs in the perennial borders to take up the space left vacant by the declining number of plants. This proved to be an ideal way to bring interest back into our garden. The types of shrubs used were all very dwarf, of several different forms. Some were deciduous and flowered; some were evergreen. Each one had some special ornamental characteristic as far as form was concerned, and, being woody plants, once they were in place, no further care was needed. The real interest came late in the fall after the tall perennials had been scythed to the ground. Formerly, when this was done, the garden was left flat and uninteresting until the bulbs bloomed in early May. But with the dwarf shrubs we had interesting forms and shapes in the garden that came into their own each fall. With winter snows there were still all sorts of odd-shaped mounds about the beds, and as the snow melted at various times between new storms the plants became visible. This lent form and considerable interest to our garden throughout the entire year. Then, with the profuse bloom of the early bulbs and the vigorous growth of the perennials, these dwarf shrubs became less and less conspicuous until the fall clean-up brought them out in the open once again.

This happy combination of bulbs, perennials, and dwarf woody plants makes for an interesting garden that is attractive every season of the year. It affords a low planting—just as low as the perennials used will grow—that can be placed where such borders or formal gardens have most value in the landscape plan and it allows you to eliminate as many annuals as you like. For those who want annuals, the space can be obtained by using fewer perennials, but the dwarf shrubs are always there to give the garden year-around interest.

One thing this combination does not do: it does not eliminate weeds. Unfortunately, they still find their way into such a planting. Though no weed killers can be used in such close quarters, mulching materials can be applied to excellent advantage. With the proper kind and amount of mulch around these perennials and shrubs, a major part of the weeding is eliminated. The weeds start, but if pulled or hoed or actually lifted out of the mulch at the right time early in their growth, weeding is reduced to an absolute minimum.

This is not to be taken as a ruthless means of eliminating all annuals and many perennials from the garden. Rather it should be understood as a suggested shortcut for those who want flower beds, but are unwilling to give the time (or the money to buy someone else's time) to care for such beds properly. Space may always be left in such beds for plants requiring time-consuming care. This method also results in beautiful formal or informal beds of flowers and low shrubs of interest throughout the entire year with a minimum amount of effort.

There are hundreds of combinations of plants that can be made, varying with the location, type of soil, and part of the country where the project is to be maintained. Any gardener can make lists of both perennials and shrubs requiring a minimum amount of attention. The lists on pages 103–193 are of bulbs, perennials, and shrubs which we have grown over the past fifteen years in a garden nearby, fully protected on all sides by hemlocks, arborvitaes, specimen trees of crab apples,

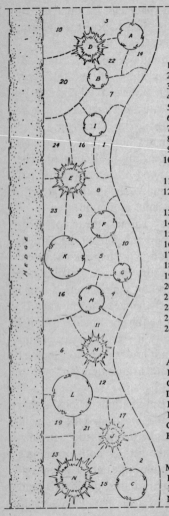

PERENNIAL-SHRUB BORDER

SCALE: |___|___|___|___|___| FEET

PERENNIALS	NO. PLANTS
1. *Ajuga reptans* 'Variegata'	24
2. *Anthemis tinctoria*	15
3. *Aster novae-angliae*	3
4. *Artemisia stelleriana*	8
5. *Cerastium tomentosum*	24
6. *Cimicifuga racemosa*	6
7. *Coreopsis auriculata* 'Nana'	18
8. *Dicentra eximia*	8
9. *Dictamnus albus*	4
10. *Filipendula vulgaris* 'Flore-pleno'	30
11. *Gaillardia aristata*	10
12. *Gypsophila paniculata* 'Bristol Fairy'	6
13. *Hemerocallis flava*	3
14. *Heuchera sanguinea*	12
15. *Hosta species and varieties*	6
16. *Lupinus polyphyllus*	6
17. *Monarda didyma*	3
18. *Miscanthus sinensis*	1
19. *Papaver orientale*	8
20. *Phlox paniculata*	6
21. *Platycodon grandiflorum*	3
22. *Sedum spectabile*	6
23. *Tanacetum vulgare*	4
24. *Yucca filamentosa*	4

SHRUBS

A. *Berberis verruculosa*
B. *Buxus* 'Kingsville'
C. *Buxus* 'Vardar Valley'
D. *Chamaecyparis obtusa* 'Compacta'
E. *Chamaecyparis pisifera* 'Filitera Nana'
F. *Ilex crenata* 'Helleri'
G. *Lavandula officinalis*
H. *Leucothoe fontanesiana*
I. *Mahonia aquifolium*
J. *Picea abies dwarf*
M. *Pieris floribunda*
K. *Pieris japonica*
L. *Taxus cuspidata* 'Aurescens'
N. *Tsuga canadensis* 'Pendula'

magnolias, dogwoods, and the like. The trees and background shrubs on three sides of this garden (approximately 130' x 300') were faced with low borders. In the center were two irregular beds stretching three-fourths the distance of the garden and surrounded with grass walks.

The combination of bulbs (those which need no attention), perennials, and shrubs, all carefully mulched (mostly with pine needles), resulted in a beautiful, low maintenance garden at all seasons of the year. Space can always be found for some new plant, or, if we remain at home throughout the summer, for a few annuals if we are willing to give the additional time required to grow them. With such a garden one's interest is retained because it does not require a continual draining of time from other activities for excessive garden work.

SHRUBS

Once the trees are located on the plan and the flower borders have been drawn in, then the shrubs can be placed. Shrubs should be chosen for the same reasons as trees—for both utilitarian and aesthetic reasons. You must know the shrub types, heights, and habits to make the right selection. Lists of shrubs which will grow under varied conditions (shade, dry soil, wet soil, etc.) are given in Chapter 3 of this book, "Low Maintenance Plants," and they are also described in greater detail in the final section where all the plants discussed in the book are listed alphabetically and described.

The main objective in choosing shrubs should be to provide for the maximum of beauty and privacy with a minimum amount of cultural care. One should consider the reason for placing every shrub on the property. Is it to create privacy, add beauty to the garden, be a background for the flower border, shield a play area, compost pile, or vegetable garden, or is it to act as a buffer between lawn and street? There should be good reason for planting every shrub used, for open space for lawn and views is also a prerequisite of a good plan. Miscellaneous shrubs in the center of the lawn can serve merely as hazards when it comes to mowing.

Be certain to select some of the dual-purpose plants (pages 145–148). If the soil is known to be dry or wet, consult these lists in order to choose the plants that will do best under such conditions. Is the shrub to grow in the shade? If so, consult the list on page 159. Are special shrubs wanted for flowering or fruiting or for colored foliage? Are evergreens wanted? All these prerequisites should be considered, and the proper lists examined in order to help with the right selections.

Be certain of the heights of the shrubs selected. Never plant taller shrubs than are needed for this always creates work; the tops will have to be continually lopped off to keep the plants in scale which usually makes them unsightly. In a shrub border, plant the taller shrubs at the rear and the smaller shrubs in the front. Allow for flower and fruiting displays at several periods in spring, summer and fall. Shrubs that are 10 to 12 feet tall should usually be planted about 10 feet apart while shrubs only 3 to 4 feet tall should be planted about 3 feet apart. If planted closer they may become too dense to flower and fruit well. On the other hand, if privacy is the factor, the taller plants might be planted closer.

Selecting the right low maintenance plant for the right place is one of the best ways of reducing garden maintenance.

FOUNDATION PLANTING

Nowhere will mistakes in plant selection be more quickly obvious than in the foundation planting about the house. The main objective here is to "tie in" the house to the soil and the surrounding vegetation—to make them an obvious part of a unit. Though few houses look well without some planting about them, too much planting, or the selection of tall-growing shrubs that quickly blot out views from windows, is a common error.

The homeowner who wants a proper foundation planting should be warned against buying smaller evergreens for such planting unless he is familiar with their rate of growth and probable height at maturity. Sometimes it is difficult to resist buying small plants that in their present form will obviously fit very well into the scale of the planting about the house. Take as an example a three-foot plant of the Moss Retinospora, which when well grown and sheared in the nursery is a perfect, soft bluish green evergreen. However, in good soil it can grow a foot a year until it is over a hundred feet tall! After it is well on its way, when its obvious tendency for growing taller and taller becomes better known, the homeowner is compelled to spend more and more time in pruning it, and it becomes more and more difficult to keep within bounds. Such is not the way to make gardening easier.

In order to make a proper foundation planting, one should know the mature heights of the plants selected, and place them accordingly. For instance, taller shrubs should be placed at the corners of the buildings, where they would not obscure the windows. If there is a porch, terrace, or patio where privacy is wanted, tall plants should be used.

Plants selected for placing in front of windows should be dwarf or very low growing, and at maturity should not reach above the bottom of a window; better still, they should grow only to a point a foot below it.

Sometimes a tall plant is wanted on either side of

an imposing main entrance, but more often medium-sized shrubs are better. Certainly for all side entrances, shrubs that mature under four feet tall are desirable.

Where windows are widely spaced, taller shrubs may be used to cover part of the bare house wall as well as to provide a contrast with the lower plants used in front of the windows. Ground covers, bulbs, and occasionally flowers may be used in front of such plants for contrast in form and color.

Foundations, depending on their height, may well be hidden with low shrubs, or even a clinging vine or two, if desired. The chimney might well be planted with a clinging vine to add contrast to the rest of the planting. A twining vine, like the Five-leaf Akebia, may be planted to wind up the rainspout or to follow a specially provided wire support to give additional height to the entire planting.

It is not correct to say that all foundation planting should be made with evergreens; usually it is more interesting to have a few deciduous flowering shrubs as well. However, because the foundation planting should be effective during the entire year, evergreens should compose a good portion of it.

The height of plants, their spacing, even open areas between them to allow for shadows and interesting contrasts in different kinds of foliage, some bulbs and deciduous plants for flower, autumn color, and fruit—all these can be blended together to make an interesting planting. If the plants mature at the proper heights, if they have been planted sufficiently far apart to give them some individuality, and if some have been selected to provide color at different times of the year, then one will have a foundation planting that will always be interesting and at the same time very easily maintained.

WOODY VINES

Vines are a necessary asset in most gardens to lend beauty and to cover objectionable walls, fences, poles, wires, and other objects. Most are fast growing, once they are started in good soil, but in selecting them one should note their respective assets carefully. Some, like the Five-leaf Akebia and Bower Actinidia are fast-growing twining vines with small flowers that are none too conspicuous.

Others are flowering vines, like wisterias, honeysuckles, and clematis. These are usually chosen for their conspicuous flowers at certain times.

The clinging vines, like English Ivy, Climbing Hydrangea, and the so-called Boston-ivy, are all useful for clinging with rootlike holdfasts to surfaces of some sort, and do not have to be helped in this clinging process by man-made aids.

The few that climb by the use of tendrils (grapes) or twining leaf stalks (clematis) of course need some supporting wires or trellis for support, and sometimes must be aided by tying the longer shoots about the supports.

Clinging vines should only be planted for growing on stone or brick walls, for on wood walls they quickly aid in the disintegration of the wood. Many a house with exterior of shingle or wood has a stone or brick chimney on the outside from ground to roof, an ideal place for some of the slower growing forms of English Ivy. For larger surfaces, the Climbing Hydrangea is excellent, for although it may take two or three years after planting to become properly established, it then becomes vigorous and will cover much space. The same is true of the Boston-ivy.

The question of how many plants to place along a wall or fence for complete coverage depends on the rapidity with which the vine grows. Usually five feet apart (or less if one is in a hurry) is about right for fast-growing vines like Boston-ivy, Climbing Hydrangea, and the Trumpet-creeper. Then if the growth is too luxuriant, some of the vines can easily be eliminated. Slower growing types like English Ivy and Creeping Fig should be planted closer together, especially for quick effects.

Twining vines should be pruned occasionally if they become too rampant or too tall. There is really no special method involved—merely cut away the excess vine foliage.

Though trellises on which to train vines are sometimes necessary, wooden ones, at least, can become a problem because they require repeated painting. A chain link fence, always effective as a barrier, can be completely and easily covered with any one of the twining vines or those with tendrils. A rainspout at a corner of the house can provide a support for properly displaying an important twining vine. If the house must be painted, the entire spout (and vine) can be laid on the ground and replaced after the painting is done. It would be easier to cut the vine off about three feet above the ground when the spout is removed; but this pruning should be done before midsummer, for if it is done later there might not be sufficient time for the plants to grow new shoots that would mature properly before freezing weather sets in.

Selecting the proper vine for the proper place is a most important operation as a labor-saver. The vines recommended in the list on page 124 are the most easily grown and cared for, and if the proper selections are made they should thrive with little attention. The method of climbing—by twining, by clinging, or by attaching themselves by means of tendrils—is all clearly marked on this list.

HEDGES—LABOR-SAVERS
UNDER SIX FEET HIGH

The old-fashioned concept of the proper hedge plant is one that is inexpensive and fast growing. In order to be inexpensive it must be easily and quickly propagated, and if it is fast growing it must be sheared frequently. Probably the most popular and widely planted hedge plant has been the California Privet, which adequately fulfills both prerequisites.

If screening alone is desired, almost any nine-foot-high shrub could be selected and several planted in a line. If such plants were allowed to go untrimmed, however, they would look ragged and unkempt. Upon examining the need for hedges more closely, it usually appears that what one really wants is a low, formal line of foliage over which one can look, through which it is difficult for animals or humans to pass, and which will appear neat at all times. If this is the kind of hedge you want, it would be a good idea to consider the new hedge plants more closely before making your final selection. There are now plants available that require very little shearing, if any, once they are established.

Without any question, the cheapest way to plant a long hedge is to use the old-fashioned, quick-growing hedge plants. But the best, low maintenance, short hedge may well be of some of the new plants that grow to a certain height and then usually maintain themselves without constant shearing. Such plants are usually slower growing than the privets and more expensive. They may be selected for their ability to produce interesting flowers or fruits, or for their fine texture or even for their informal, regular habit of growth when left unsheared.

The more "informal" appearing the hedge can be, the less shearing will be required, with certain plants.

Others, like the dwarf forms of Japanese Barberry, are mounded in general habit, and always look as if they have been sheared when actually they have not.

There are some plants—like the Dwarf Eastern Ninebark—which, if used in a hedge, could be allowed to grow "informally," that is, unsheared, for as long as desired. This would result in a rather wide, fan-shaped type of hedge that could be most interesting because of its increased flowering and fruiting (when compared to what it would be like sheared) and also because of the graceful nodding of the upright branches in the wind. Such an informal growth would result in a wide hedge, probably as wide as tall. If this proved to be too wide, or if one wished the more "formal" sheared type of hedge, it could be easily and quickly attained merely by shearing the plants to the proper dimensions. In this way, with certain plants, one can have a "formal" (sheared) or an "informal" (flowering and fruiting) hedge at will.

In planning where to place the hedge, one should keep in mind that it never should be exactly on the property line, always a foot or so inside. The abutting property owner has the right to cut off or dig up any part of the hedge which encroaches on his side of the line. It is best to dig a ditch about 18 inches wide and 1½ feet deep, removing poor soil and replacing it with good soil. Hedge plants might best be bought 2 to 3 feet tall, but as noted above, larger sizes can be used if necessary. The reason for the smaller plants is that they cost less and are easier to establish.

Spaced 1½ to 3 feet apart, the deciduous types can be cut to within 6 to 12 inches of the soil immediately after planting. This is hard for many gardeners to do, but it forces the plants to send out new buds and shoots from near the base of the plant, thus making a dense hedge. Tall, spindly plants may eventually grow into a hedge, but they will be open at the bottom, allowing animals to go through. Another way to overcome this same hazard is to run a line of chicken wire, 2 to 3 feet tall, along the newly planted hedge line. This will help keep out animals and the wire can be left indefinitely, eventually rusting out as the plants grow thicker.

When pruning or shearing is necessary, the hedge should always be narrow at the top, wider at the base, thus allowing the valuable lower branches to develop properly with sufficient sunlight. If shearing is to be done (and some of the rounded hedge plants mentioned in the list on pages 136–140 do not require it), hedges are best trimmed just as their growth is nearly complete, usually in early June, a few weeks later with the evergreens.

Evergreen hedges are not as quick to recuperate from heavy pruning; hence they should not be cut back so severely at the start, merely lightly trimmed.

Hedges such as the red-leaved 'Crimson Pygmy' Barberry, 'Curly Locks' Box, 'Helleri' Japanese Holly and the Cushioned Japanese Yew, only need a "touching up" with the shears once every two or three years. More vigorous hedges like the Slender Deutzia, *Philadelphus* 'Avalanche' and *Viburnum opulus* 'Compactum' may need a shearing once a year, but these can also be allowed to grow (and flower and fruit) at will, without any shearing for a few years, to make delightfully informal hedges. Later they can be formally sheared if desired.

Study the list of labor-saving hedge plants on pages 136–140 and select some of these slow-growing low types that will make excellent hedges under the eye level in height. To plant fast-growing hedge plants (when the mature height is to be under the eye level) is only asking for more and more maintenance work.

VEGETABLES

If a vegetable garden is needed, it is possible that it will eventually outlive its usefulness; at which time, it may be seeded over and used for some other purpose.

In the midwinter planning season the idea of a vegetable garden seems attractive, but during midsummer, when the constant fight against drought, poor soil, weeds, insects, and disease is at its height, many people tend to have second thoughts. We have had a vegetable garden each summer for many, many years, varying in size from 50 feet x 100 feet to 100 feet x 300 feet, which you must admit is a sizable plot. With youngsters at home to care for it, there were not too many problems except to keep after the youngsters. When we had to do all the work ourselves, we drastically reduced the size of the garden.

Now we say each year that it is not worth the effort, modern packaging and frozen-food products being what they are. However, in the winter, when "spring-fever planting" has control of both of us, we usually again plan to plant more than we can use. Everyone must make his own decision on the merits of a vegetable garden. If, however, a vegetable garden is decided on, but you don't enjoy the work of it, take a tip from an old hand who has grown everything from peanuts to soybeans, and plant only the easy things like carrots, beans, corn, and tomatoes.

It is obvious that the size of the vegetable garden depends upon one's needs, the space available, and one's willingness to care for it. A vegetable garden 25 feet x 50 feet, if properly planned, can supply four people with vegetables from June to October, but the gardener looking for shortcuts is certainly not going to be bogged down with growing his own vegetables. If he is interested, the state experiment station has excellent free bulletins giving information about planting the right kind of garden in the right way.

FRUITS

Bush fruits are another addition to the home planting, but the size of the space available determines whether or not these are planted. For instance, one or two raspberry bushes would take up valuable space in a small garden, and all the fruits may well be taken by the birds. If space is available for twenty-five plants (about two to three feet apart in the row) without using land needed for more important assignments, then plan on the raspberries by all means. But remember: the fruits must be picked and the plants pruned, and all that is real work!

Fruit trees are interesting to read about in colorful catalogues, but such publications usually neglect to remind you that in order to bear suitable fruits such trees must be thoroughly sprayed four to seven times during the growing season at just the right times. Take the McIntosh apple as an example—this year these apples were selling at wayside stands in New England for $4.00 and up per bushel. If you are thinking of saving money by growing your own fruits, take a second look at the facts before you give up valuable space to this activity. If it is an interesting hobby you want, although often expensive and discouraging during the years the trees fail to fruit, plant the tree fruits; but if you wish to save labor, omit them from the planting scheme.

We like strawberries, blueberries, and grapes, and have the space to grow them and are willing to give the time and energy to do so successfully. When such fruits are grown and enjoyed, gardening is a real hobby. But they do require maintenance work.

SPECIAL PROBLEMS

Any garden may have special needs that have to be considered—possibly a rock garden or a hedge must be located, or a bank of rocky soil properly planned for in the easiest possible way. Are there any unsightly views that should be screened out with tall shrubs or trees? If the garage is separate from the house, should it be shielded with shrubs or a vine trellis? Are any permanent stone seats or small statues to be located and properly placed? If there are permanent walks, are they to be paved, or are stepping-stones and gravel sufficient?

Very important, too, is to remember to allow for easy access to every part of the property: leave room for trucks to deliver coal or oil; have a place for stacking wood, if fireplaces are to be used; and, what is more important (and often overlooked), if any trucking is to be done over the property (of manure, soil, stone, coal, wood, and so on), always leave space available for such passage at the most strategic places. The smaller the garden, the more one should give careful consideration to the possibility of the movement on the property at some time in the future.

Finally, the question often arises—how should one obtain local advice. The novice can, if he prefers, go to his local landscape architect or to his nurseryman, if he is one who has talented landscape advice available. To the experienced individual, or the one who has had considerable plant training, such advice may not be needed. Or one can refer to various reference books, articles, and experiment station publications, all of which should be studied carefully to sift all the pertinent facts concerning the type of planting desired. For those planning a garden for the first time, professional advice at the beginning sometimes saves many a headache and much money later on. For others who like to learn from their own mistakes, planning their own place is a challenge. Regardless of which attitude is taken, it pays to consider carefully all these items in advance, on paper, before any actual plantings are made. In other words, first have a plan, and make certain that it is the best possible one that can be devised. Once the plan has been decided on, try to stay with it and avoid costly, last-minute changes. Undoubtedly, having a good plan before planting is one of the best shortcuts to having a successful and easily cared for garden.

HOW TO USE THE HARDINESS MAPS

The Hardiness Maps included in this book make it easy for you to come to a quick decision about which plants can be grown in your area. All plants in this book have been given a hardiness rating geared to these maps.

Plant hardiness is a highly complex factor, and depends on temperature, rainfall, and soil. Since it is impossible to show these three variables simply for an area as large as the United States, the best practical method is to show hardiness ratings on the basis of average annual minimum temperatures. This gives a fairly accurate idea of where certain plants will grow, and is the method used satisfactorily by the author in other reference books as well as here.

Those familiar with hardiness zones realize that altitude plays its part too; the higher up a tall mountain one goes, the lower the average annual minimum temperature and hence the fewer plants that can be grown. The zone number given for the plants discussed in this book does not indicate that they can only be grown in the one band across the land; they may be grown in a colder zone, but only with a great deal of protection.

They can also be grown in several warmer zones, at least until rainfall, summer heat, and possibly soil conditions become limiting factors.

To use the maps to best advantage, first determine the hardiness zone in which you live. Then, in checking the lists and noting the hardiness zone numbers for each plant, you can see at a glance what plants you should expect to grow. If, for instence, you live in the Boston, Massachusetts area, you should be able to grow all plants listed for Zone 5. Also, it is very important to remember, you can also grow all plants listed for colder zones, i.e. Zones 2, 3, and 4. As for the plants listed in the next warmer zone, i.e. Zone 6, you might be able to grow a few of them, but they would require a great deal of winter protection. They might survive some winters and be killed by others. It would be practically worthless to attempt to grow plants listed for still warmer zones, i.e. Zones 7 to 9.

The hardiness zone ratings are not infallible, but they are a means of telling in advance, with a reasonable degree of accuracy, the plants that can be grown in any certain area. This of course saves much effort in hit-or-miss experimental maintenance.

2
_____

Shortcuts and
Aids in Maintenance

The modern gardener can take advantage of the many shortcuts and aids to gardening that are available today. Centuries of growing plants by dedicated gardeners everywhere has resulted in volumes of information. Modern engineering and chemistry both contribute their full share of aid. Plant explorers have searched the world for new and better plants. Government experiment stations throughout America annually make sizeable appropriations for experimental work, research which helps the homeowner with his own gardening problems. In effect, the modern gardener can, if he wishes, materially reduce expense and personal labor by using these many sources now available to him.

In approaching low maintenance gardening, there are three basic factors to consider. Planning, the first and often the most important element, has already been discussed. Garden shortcuts and aids will be discussed in this section. Finally, the selection of the right low maintenance plants that are now available to the public (or soon will be) for specific situations is taken up in the third main section of this book.

Few gardeners will want to avail themselves of all these shortcuts, and the majority may not wish to confine themselves to growing only the low maintenance plants discussed in the last section. All, however, will find herein some information of value to them in making low maintenance gardening a more pleasant and interesting experience.

PLANTING

The objective in every planting is to have healthy, well-grown plants that are always in vigorous condition. You will not, I'm afraid, find any shortcuts at planting time. Many years ago, L. H. Bailey said that it was always better to prepare a five dollar hole for a fifty-cent shrub rather than to plant a five-dollar shrub in a fifty-cent hole. There is a great deal of truth in this; far too often, with plants just obtained from the nursery, one hurries to plant them quickly to finish the job.

It is far better to prepare the holes for the plants in advance and thus to find out the kind of soil where the plants are to be permanently placed. If it is poor—composed chiefly of gravel or very sandy soil—it should be removed to a depth of at least 18 inches, depending on the size of plant used; with trees or large balled evergreens the soil may have to be excavated deeper. The hole should be at least two feet wider than the roots of the new plant, so that when the roots are placed normally in the hole they can be comfortably spread out (not jammed in together) and have a foot on all sides in which to enlarge properly.

Well-rotted manure or decomposed compost might be placed in the bottom of the hole, two inches of soil added on top, and the plant carefully set in the hole on top of that. Then good soil is firmed in about the normally spread-out roots, and a slight depression left at the top of the hole to catch and hold water until the plant becomes fully established. Care should be taken not to plant when the soil is muddy, for in firming such soil it may dry out into an almost bricklike consistency. Also, the young plants should be set out at exactly the same depth they were in the nursery row prior to digging. When planting is completed, then in order to keep the young plants from drying out during the first years of growth, they should be properly mulched. See Mulching (p. 57).

WATERING

The young plants should be thoroughly watered in at once—really soaked in—and water applied to them when necessary during the *next two years* so that at no time does the soil actually dry out in periods of drought.

The use of water wands (gadgets that permit water to leak out without the force or pressure that one finds in an open hose) are ideal. Soil soakers—long, porous hoses that when attached to a hose allow the water to ooze out slowly—are also excellent. A good deal of water is needed to soak into the soil to reach a depth of 12 to 18 inches, and when applied by "pressure" watering, much of it quickly runs off. In fact, letting the water soak slowly into the soil, by either of these two methods, or by the use of sprinklers kept in one position for a long time, is the best method of watering anything whether it be lawn, newly planted shrubbery, or a flower bed.

The gardener who makes a big show of watering with a pressure hose, going quickly from one spot to the next, is really wasting time as well as water. Water applied in this fashion seldom goes into the soil more than a fraction of an inch, and because it is on the surface, it quickly evaporates without even reaching the roots of the plants. It is a good idea to test the method you use, timing the soaker or sprinkler, and then digging into the soil to see how far the water has penetrated, since soils differ in the rapidity with which they soak up water. To be effective, the water must get down to the plant roots.

There may be places about the grounds where water outlets would be a most desirable asset. It is not necessary to use metal pipe for these outlets, which must be either drained in the fall or else installed below the frost line. The best modern shortcut is to use plastic pipe. It is a good idea to set these in the ground so that they can be drained, but this is not necessary. They need be inserted only a few inches below the soil level, and once in the ground they can last for many years without breaking. They are highly practical and economical as well.

Various watering devices are available in all makes and types. We even fell for an ad which asked, if there was a rectangular bed, why waste water? The obvious thing to do was to buy the device advertised, which spread water on the ground in a regulated rectangular pattern. We bought it; but later we realized that any device with a back-and-forth motion does the same thing, and can be regulated by the amount of water pressure.

Watering, like planting, should be done with care, and if done correctly will be worth the time expended. If done with "a lick and a promise" the time and money can be considered wasted.

BANK PLANTING

The chief objective in bank planting is to select vigorous-growing species which will root along procumbent stems on or near the soil surface. This will tend to hold the soil in place and keep it from washing away during heavy rains. Many banks are unsuitable for growing grass; either the gradient is too steep or the soil is irregular and covered with rocks and large boulders, making it difficult or impossible to maintain a lawn.

The soil on the bank should be as good as possible. Mix in compost or well-rotted leaves or manure. If the soil is very sandy, add peat moss to help the soil retain moisture.

If grass must be planted, there are roughly woven, light burlaplike rolls of open-mesh woven material available that can be laid and then pegged down over the seeding. This is left on to eventually rot away. It ensures a good start for the grass by keeping the soil from washing away in rains until the grass becomes firmly established. If the grade is too steep for this, and grass must be grown, then sods of grass should be laid down. These are bought in rolls of living grass and pegged down to keep them in place at the start, but one should remember that the gradient can become too steep to mow any grass properly, regardless of how it is started. Recognizing such situations for what they are, and planting bank plants instead of grass, results in low maintenance later.

Often it is easiest in the long run to forget growing grass on banks and use fast-growing bank plants selected from the list (pages 134–135). Plant well, in good-sized holes, and space the plants so they will give a reasonably good cover in two or three years. The Memorial Rose, as one example, is fast growing, rambles over rocks and boulders, and its rooting can be hastened if a few shovelsful of soil are placed over the longer runners to aid rooting at those places. The plants should be spaced 3 to 4 feet apart.

Junipers might be planted 2 to 3 feet apart; Forsythia 'Arnold Dwarf' and *Stephanandra incisa* 'Crispa' about the same. This last is an excellent new plant for bank planting and can be easily pruned back to any height if it grows too high. Periwinkle clumps on the other hand might be spaced a foot or less apart. The nursery or garden center where the plants are purchased can save problems later by telling you how far apart to space the plants chosen.

After planting and watering well, then mulch (see Mulching, p. 57) for mulching is a necessity on any bank planting. This mulch should be periodically renewed whenever needed. It is the best low-maintenance insurance on bank plantings for it aids in keeping the soil moist and the plants growing.

Soil, soil mixture, steepness of the bank, and the speed with which a cover is needed, all govern the type of plant selected and the planting distances to be used for bank planting.

SHADE PLANTING

Trying to grow plants in the shade can be a frustrating experience. Shade can vary from continual light shade to intermittent shade caused by buildings, to very dense continual shade. The deeper the shade, the fewer the plants which will survive.

Shade caused by low, overhanging tree branches is also accompanied by tree roots close to the surface of the soil which can have a serious effect on the growth of plants. The roots of Norway Maples and beech trees, as examples, will absorb most of the available moisture and nutrients, so that plants placed beneath them have little chance to grow normally.

Under such circumstances instead of experimenting with different plants and suffering successive losses, select a few of the sturdiest in the list of plants withstanding shade (pages 158–162), such as Japanese Pachysandra, barberries, or yews. If they fail, simply give up the situation as too difficult. Spread crushed stone over the area, or use paving stones. There are some situations where plant growing is practically impossible, and the sooner one recognizes such situations for what they are, the more time one will have to devote to more rewarding areas of the garden.

All the plants in the list on pages 158–162 will withstand some shade, some more than others. One can select several types that would be suitable and worthy of trial. Give them the best of soil, moisture, and fertilizer conditions to offset the growth-slowing effect of the shade. A little effort in properly selecting plants for the shaded areas about the home grounds will definitely result in low maintenance later.

GROUND COVERS

Ground covers are low, woody, or herbaceous plants that grow rapidly and are dense enough to cover bare ground. Only a very few are considered substitutes for a grass lawn, since few of them can survive being walked on. There are areas in most gardens where a low ground cover is most useful—in the shade (page 158); in dry areas (page 151); in wet soil (page 155); on a bank (page 134)—in fact any place where it is difficult or undesirable to maintain grass. Extreme care should be made to select the correct type of ground cover initially. Know its height, what it looks like, whether it's evergreen, and whether it will grow in the site selected. Quick information about these will be found in the alphabetical listing (pages 197–358) and also on pages 127–133.

The majority of the low maintenance ground covers in the list (pages 127–133) can be grown in the full sun; thirty-one will withstand partial shade, and these are marked with an (S).

Good soil is a necessity and the best way to provide it is when the initial planting is made. Remove poor soil, to a depth of 4 to 6 inches, depending on the size of the plant, and then provide good top soil. Mix in well-decomposed humus or rotted leaves, compost or manure, even peat moss if there is nothing better, as this aids the soil in retaining moisture. Also, if necessary, mix in a fertilizer recommended by the nurseryman or garden center, but be sure to read the directions on the bag so you will know how much to apply. A "complete" fertilizer of the granular chemical kind labeled 5–10–5 (5 percent nitrogen, 10 percent phosphoric acid and 5 percent potash) is often available. This could be mixed with the soil before planting at 3 to 5 pounds per hundred square feet. If the best possible soil is given at the start, the ground cover will grow quickly and can be expected to be truly low maintenance.

Spacing the plants depends, of course, on the kind of plants selected. Many of the herbaceous plants could be spaced one per square foot, but Hostas might easily be allowed 2 square feet for each plant. Vigorous plants like the Memorial Rose and junipers might be allowed 3 to 4 square feet at the start. The pachysandras, thymes, and bugleweed might be spaced only 6 inches apart, especially if a quick cover is desired. Get approximate planting distances from the store where you buy plants. This prevents problems later!

Mulching the new bed is always an excellent way to reduce maintenance later for it reduces weed growth and water loss from the soil. See Mulching (page 57) for full information.

Do not let the new planting dry out during the first year of summer droughts. Winter protection, especially through the first winter, is a must. This can take the form of a good mulch, or possibly pine boughs or straw thrown lightly over the plants to protect them from too much winter sun and the alternate freezing and thawing of the soil in the winter which sometimes results in actually pushing the young plants out of the soil. If this occurs, they should be replanted immediately.

Fertilizing after the first winter sometimes may be helpful. Apply the fertilizer before the plants start growth in the spring, at rates recommended on the container. Water the fertilizer at once so that none remains on the foliage. Many find the easiest way of fertilizing is by use of a fertilizer cartridge attached to the garden hose. If this method is chosen, the directions with the cartridge should be followed exactly.

The quickest possible way to save time, trouble, and expense is to take time at the start to select the right ground cover for the right place. Then plant in good soil, mulch well, and keep the soil from drying out.

LAWN SUBSTITUTES

There are many homeowners seeking shortcuts to having a good lawn. It should be emphatically stated at the start that there is no material that will appear as neat or be as serviceable as good, well-cut grass. True, it must be cared for—fertilized, watered, and cut—but if these things are carried out well there is no plant better suited for lawns than grass. There are different kinds of grasses and different grass mixtures for varying situations, but all require reasonable care in order to look well. Given this care, they serve indefinitely.

There is always the perfectionist who never can rest until every dandelion seedling and every bit of Crab Grass has been painfully pulled from his lawn. He spends all his spare time on his hands and knees, and welcomes visitors in order to inveigle them into helping him. If he enjoys this, it is probably satisfactory for him, but it can certainly discourage visitors!

About the only shortcut in lawn maintenance is to acquire the state of mind that enables one to see all the good things about the lawn, while at the same time overlooking completely its many little shortcomings. For instance, the lawn never looks better than in the early spring. The first task is to fertilize, a process that invariably results in a greener lawn, faster growing grass, and hence more labor in cutting. Can one be satisfied with a second-rate lawn requiring less maintenance time—that is, no fertilizer—or must one aim for the best, year after year? It is a momentous question that every gardener will have to answer for himself.

Weekly cutting, or approximately that, is another hurdle. Closer cutting makes for a more uniform lawn but it does take time. Can the gardener be satisfied with higher grass in the lawn, cut every two weeks, possibly with little piles of clippings left here and there? These piles turn brown as they die and can be so dense that they kill small spots of grass underneath. Can the owner bring himself to a state of mind where such a lawn doesn't bother him? Admittedly, if the lawn is in an inconspicuous place, less cutting may well be the rule.

When weeds like dandelion and Crab Grass begin to take over, is the gardener going to approve of the different color scheme and note the advantage of such a lawn, or is he going to fret until every last weed is pulled? All depends on the individual, and one might as well take stock of one's self and one's projected lawn before it is even planted, to try to predetermine the hazards of maintenance from the psychological point of view.

As old hands at gardening, both my wife and I have been through all phases of lawn maintenance. There used to be a time when every weed was religiously pulled, fertilizing was done every spring, and summer watering was a welcomed recreation. As time went on, and we learned that most of the summer droughts in our area did not actually kill the grass although they could mar it for some time, we came to the satisfying point of view that we were going to appreciate the change of appearance in our lawn from one season to another. I do not mean that we allowed dandelions to take over, but we took out the majority—if we wanted to or could inveigle one of the children to do it; otherwise we would try (if we had time and did not forget) some of the weed killers especially made to eliminate dandelions. If we remembered and did it—fine! But if we forgot or went on a trip when the work should have been done— that was also fine! Then we would be most interested in seeing what would happen to the lawn because we had not pampered it at the proper time. As the years rolled on, we learned how to compliment our friends on their beautiful lawns, and became satisfied in allowing ours to be the one they used for comparison. They liked that (and had the work). We also liked it, because it made them happy and we didn't have the work. We found that the lawn would not die. One summer we went away and left it for ten weeks without mowing. Fortunately, there was a drought, but even if there had not been, that lawn was due for a real labor-saving experiment. Admittedly, it looked pretty bad on our return, but the grass did not die (much) and then we had the pleasure of seeing how fast it recuperated with a minimum of care. So, a state of mind is the best shortcut to lawn maintenance.

Because lawns are being maintained under many and varied situations in this vast country, it is impossible to make all-inclusive statements about plants that might be used as grass substitutes. Under certain conditions, especially in the southern parts of the country, there has been a great demand for Zoysia grasses of one clone or another. These are more uniform and slower in growth and need less care. Zoysia lawns are planted by seed (2 pounds per 1000 square feet), sprigs, or plugs and the resulting lawns are so dense and tough that it is best to have heavy-duty, reel-type mowers. In the North, Zoysia turns brown in the winter after the first heavy frost and remains brown all winter. This makes it unsightly as well as a fire hazard, while a good stand of Kentucky Bluegrass usually remains green all winter long.

Dichondra repens is a lawn substitute widely used in the southwestern United States, but only in areas where winter temperatures do not go below 25°F. It is not a grass but a creeping broad-leaved perennial plant, a native of the West Indies, with small leaves less than one-quarter inch in diameter. A Dichondra lawn can either be started by seeding or by planting plugs of the growing plant. Seed is used at the rate of 2 pounds per 1000 square feet, preferably sown between March and May. It should not be sown in mixtures and does not need a nurse crop. If planted in plugs, these should be spaced 6 to 12 inches apart. However, a Dichondra lawn does need nearly as much attention as a grass lawn, although if it is in hot sun, with people walking on it continually, the times between mowing can be considerably longer than with a grass lawn.

Then there are the Lily-turf species (*Liriope*) which have been widely advertised as lawn substitutes. Unfortunately, many advertisements leave the uninitiated with the impression that these plants are the real answer to a lawn substitute. Here again, in certain areas of the South they may have their place, but most are not suitable for continued growth in the northern gardens of the United States. One species, *Liriope spicata,* is hardy in the North, but anyone who has grown it knows that if Quack Grass ever gets into a planting of *Liriope spicata* the entire area must be dug up and the Quack Grass deliberately separated from the Lily-turf, piece by piece, and the latter then replanted.

Over the years other types of plants have been tried in various areas with questionable success: Sandworts (*Arenaria* species); Roman Camomile (*Anthemis nobilis*); Common Yarrow (*Achillea millefolium*); Brassbuttons (*Cotula* species); Mayweed (*Matricaria* species); Procumbent Pearlwort (*Sagina procumbens*). Others have been given a certain amount of publicity, but when investigated carefully it has usually appeared that any success has been obtained in small local areas, under extremely local climatic conditions. For instance, one gardener on Nantucket Island off the southern Massachusetts coast became very discouraged with his grass lawn, for it usually dried up during the summer months in the sandy soil unless it was watered with unfailing regularity. Experimenting with a small spot of yarrow, he found that this plant could be cut with a lawn mower and that it would result in a fairly green surface during hot summer droughts without incessant watering. Later, he sowed his entire lawn with yarrow. He was rightly proud of his green "lawn" when those all about him were brown in summer. However, the atmospheric moisture was undoubtedly high in this small area, even though rainfall was deficient, and yarrow is apparently a plant able to utilize atmospheric moisture far better than many grasses. In areas where this atmospheric moisture is not available, a yarrow "lawn" might well have its drawbacks during serious summer droughts.

Local soils and climatic conditions, therefore, play an extremely important part in the success or failure of lawn substitutes. A certain amount of experimentation by the gardener, especially on small plots of a hundred square feet, may prove most helpful to him in making a later decision concerning what to plant in his lawn. In no case, however, should he plant thousands of square feet of a "lawn substitute" without first studying carefully all the good and bad points about it in his particular local area. Rather than waste too much energy and expense experimenting on large areas with plants of unknown performance, it would be much wiser to admit that, with all its faults, the right kind of grass creates the fastest growing and most serviceable lawn.

PRUNING

One of the best shortcuts to maintaining a home planting easily is to understand the few simple rudiments of pruning, and to prune—where necessary—early in the life of the shrub or tree. This saves major work later on. A small sapling eight feet tall (or less) showing a double leader should have one of the leaders removed as soon as it is first noticed, otherwise the fault will be growing bigger year by year until correcting it may easily become a costly major operation, whereas a snip of the hand shears in the first place would have done the job satisfactorily.

A little knowledge of what to prune and how to do it goes a very long way in helping plants grow into well-balanced specimens that are an asset in any garden. Conversely, the indiscriminate hacking of shrubs and trees at definite heights is the quickest means by which otherwise beautiful plantings are made unsightly. Here are a few of the general essentials:

As far as the growth of the plant is concerned,

40

pruning can be done at almost any time except in the early summer, for if done then, the new growth may not have sufficient time to mature before winter, and killing may result. However, as far as our interest in the ornamental qualities of plants is concerned, shrubs are divided into two groups, first, those that bloom in the early spring, like daphne, forsythia, and lilac, which might be pruned after they flower in order to obtain the full benefit of their flower the current year; and second, plants that bloom on the current year's wood, like hydrangea and Rose of Sharon, which can be pruned in the late winter or early spring and still be expected to bloom the same year. Trees are usually pruned in the late winter and early spring (with the exception of those that "bleed" profusely, like the birch, maple, or Yellowwood), for at this time, before the leaves appear, it is much easier to see which branches should be removed, and also it gives the tree the entire spring and summer to form new growth.

What to Prune

1. Dead, broken, or diseased branches.
2. Broken roots and one-third of the branches at transplanting time. Some roots are always cut when a plant is dug. A good general rule is to remove about one-third of the total linear branch length, when the plant is moved, by thinning out weak or damaged branches and correcting structural defects. This compensates for the loss of roots that have been cut in the transplanting operation, and always results in more vigorous plants at the end of the first year. This is difficult for the homeowner to do, since the new plant looks smaller than the original specimen purchased from the nursery, but it is always better for the plant in the end. When plants are to be moved from their native place in the

woods, it is advisable to root-prune (merely forcing a spade in the ground in a wide circle about the plant) one year in advance, to force the production of many roots close to the base so that the transplanting operation will be easier. Nursery-grown plants are usually root-pruned periodically.

3. Young trees should be pruned early. Timely corrective pruning saves trouble later. If the tree is one that normally has a single trunk, see that only one straight trunk develops and cut out any others that try to grow. Occasionally several branches grow out from the trunk at the same place, and these will always make weak crotches. All but one should be removed. Sometimes young shrubs should be "headed back" a bit to force them to grow more branches from the base. A forsythia, for instance, with just one leader would never become an interesting shrub. In other words, know how the tree or shrub will develop at maturity, and help it early in life by selecting the proper leaders, removing the others if necessary.

4. Correct structural defects. Never allow two equally vigorous leaders to develop on exactly opposite sides of the same trunk. This will always be a "weak" crotch, susceptible to splitting as the tree grows older. It may spoil the symmetry of the entire tree when this happens. There are several kinds of weak crotches to look for, but in general the greater the angle a branch makes where it leaves the trunk of the tree, the stronger the wood at that union. It is really very simple to watch the younger trees as they begin to grow, and with hand shears quickly remove secondary leaders, unnecessary crossing branches, and so on.

5. Cut suckers from the bases of grafted or budded plants. Many plants used in gardens, such as roses, crab apples, lilacs, and fruit trees, are either grafted or budded on another kind of understock. Usually, this is

never more than a foot or so from the ground. Hence, all suckers developing below this point should be removed as soon as they are observed, for if allowed to develop they will not only spoil the symmetry of the plant and sap the strength of the variety wanted, but will develop into an entirely different and usually undesirable plant. Roses especially produce frequent examples of understock growth, since many an ornamental rose is budded or grafted on *Rosa multiflora* as an understock. This is a vigorous-growing rose species, and once started into growth above ground it quickly takes over the entire plant. Frequently, when two kinds of blossoms or leaves are seen on one plant this is the reason. The understock suckers should be cut out as soon as they develop.

6. Rejuvenate old shrubs. A Mock-orange, privet, lilac, spirea, or many another shrub may grow too tall and become open and ungainly at the base. Most shrubs can be rejuvenated in one of two ways: either by cutting the entire shrub to six inches above the ground in the early spring and allowing it to develop as a new plant; or by thinning out the old wood, cutting some of the older branches off near the ground and allowing new ones to form, then repeating the process with a few more of the older branches the second and third years. Lilacs are often treated thus, for in this way they produce a few blooms each year of the change, while when they are cut to the ground they do not bloom for two or three years. Forsythias, privets, Mock-oranges, deutzias, and even lilacs treated in this way early one spring have flowered the following year. Usually one must wait another year or two for such shrubs to bloom when they have been cut back hard. It is essential to note, however, that many evergreens do not respond to such drastic pruning, although a few may. To be on the safe side, one should follow the general rule that evergreens should

be thinned but not be expected to grow back to good size if cut to the ground. Certainly few if any of the conifers will recuperate and reproduce new shoots when cut to the ground.

7. Hedges, screens, and windbreaks. These should be pruned with the objective of increasing their density, for if a twig is cut back a few inches it frequently sends out more than one new shoot to take the place of the one removed. This growth habit of plants can be utilized to force them to grow more dense.

8. Certain limbs for utility purposes. The lower limbs of street trees, or limbs that interfere with a certain view, walk, window or wire, must sometimes be removed.

9. Girdling root. Close observation of the base of trees which are growing poorly often discloses a girdling root; that is, a root partly on the surface of the soil or just beneath, that is growing in such a way as to choke or constrict the trunk of the tree or a larger root. Such girdling roots can do real harm and usually should be cut as near as possible to the trunk of the tree or at least at the point where they are doing the damage.

These, then, are the reasons for pruning. Be certain the reason for pruning is understood before it is done, for it is always a dwarfing process, and there are some plants that never need any. Study the situation and have a good reason for all pruning.

How to Prune

1. Make all cuts clean, with sharp tools.
2. Never leave any stubs. A short stub may never heal over and is always a source of infection. Make all cuts back to a bud, branch, or main trunk. The removal of a large limb should be done in 3 cuts. First, an undercut is made on the bottom of the branch by sawing up

one-fourth or one-third through the limb about a foot from the trunk of the tree. Then the upper cut is started on the top of the branch, one to two inches beyond the first cut but toward the trunk, and sawed down until the limb falls. As the two cuts near each other and the limb begins to sag, its weight will break the wood at the center and the limb will jump clear without stripping and tearing the bark down the tree trunk. Finally, the stump is removed by a cut flush with the trunk of the tree.

3. Paint all cuts over 1 inch to 2 inches in diameter with a special protective tree paint.

4. Disinfect tools after each cut on a diseased plant. A satisfactory disinfectant to have in a suitable can for this purpose is alcohol.

5. Shrub rejuvenation. Thin out the older branches over a period of a few years or cut the shrub to within a few inches of the ground in late winter or early spring. The obvious exception to this would be weak-growing shrubs or those which have been budded or grafted. Never cut any shrub off at a horizontal line several feet above the ground. This is an artificial practice outmoded for many years, and always results in unsightly specimens. Thin out here and there, cut one branch back hard and another not nearly so much, and thin out from the base simultaneously. In this way an old plant can be reduced in size, still look natural, and will produce new growth at different places from the ground on up to the top.

6. Shear hedges wider at the base than the top. Both evergreen and deciduous hedges should be sheared in such a way that they are wider at the base than at the top, thus allowing the important lower branches plenty of room, light, and air. If the hedge is pruned narrower at the base than at the top, the lower branches will often die from lack of light. Once these lower branches die on an evergreen hedge, it is practically

impossible to force any new ones to grow in the same place. Deciduous hedges, on the other hand, are mostly vigorous-growing plants, and when they become open at the base the entire hedge can be cut to within a few inches of the ground in the early spring and will quickly start a new, vigorous growth from the ground, thus forming a new hedge in a few years' time.

Pruning need not be difficult. It is important, however, that one understand exactly why the contemplated pruning is necessary and can visualize the probable results. Even yews and rhododendrons can be heavily pruned and old plants rejuvenated by the expert gardener who has previously studied what to do and when to do it.

FERTILIZING

Fertilizers are applied to make plants grow more vigorously and so to produce more leaf, stem, flower, root, and fruit. This should be remembered especially in fertilizing the lawn, for more growth means frequent grass cutting. With certain foundation plants, such as Canada Hemlocks that are to be restrained to six feet, more growth may create more work in pruning. More growth can certainly produce more work in shearing a hedge. Think twice before fertilizers are used, especially if garden labor is to be cut to a minimum.

At one time, before chemical fertilizers were developed, manure was the fertilizer most commonly used in gardening. If you live in a suburban community where manure is free or cheaply available, it is a most valuable aid to cultivation; like other organic matter, such as decomposing weeds, leaves, and so on, it releases available nitrogen and other nutrients into the soil as well as aiding the water-retention properties of the soil. It should be remembered, however, that a ton of average manure contains about the same amounts of nitrogen and potash as 100 pounds of 5–10–5 commercial fertilizer (5 parts nitrogen, 10 parts phosphoric acid, and 5 parts potash), although only about one-fourth as much phosphate. If manure is not available, a combination of rotting vegetable compost complemented with commercial fertilizer can achieve the same end results.

Tilth is frequently aided by the addition of organic matter to the soil; and usually manure, and commercial fertilizers as well, contain a certain amount of other elements that sometimes are deficient in the soil. Certainly one cannot have a vegetable garden on the same plot year in and year out, annually taking off crops of vegetables, without replenishing the soil with fertilizers in some way. Farmers practice crop rotation; the amateur vegetable gardener with only limited space must be satisfied with the simple addition of organic manures or commercial fertilizers.

Unquestionably, the proper application of the right kind of fertilizer at the right time is one of the easiest aids to insure vigorous plant growth. Many gardeners who are in a hurry fail to take the time to determine the proper amount or the proper kind of fertilizer to apply at any one time, and as a result of their efforts they may do more harm to the plants than good. There are a few simple fundamentals one should understand before applying large amounts of fertilizers to plants. These will be briefly summed up for the benefit of those who wish to review the subject.

Most plants grow in soil, and in the soils there are usually some 15 elements. Many of these are termed "trace" elements or "minor" elements, since they are usually present in most soils in minute quantities but sufficient for plant growth. The most important elements needed in the largest amounts for plant growth are nitrogen, phosphorus, and potassium. It is these that are the chief components of the so-called "commercial" fertilizer in the 5–10–5 ratio noted above.

Water in the soil (and in the atmosphere), warm temperatures, and light are also necessary ingredients for plant growth. In gardens out of doors we cannot do much about the temperature; we try to segregate those plants requiring some shade from those that will withstand full sun; and of course we can augment the water that comes from the skies in the form of rain.

Plants vary in their requirements for water, in their ability to withstand continually high temperatures and, as just pointed out, in the amount of direct sunlight they can withstand. Therefore, it is obvious why all plants cannot grow in all locations, even though the soil might be uniform, which of course it is not.

Presupposing that plants to be grown in a certain soil are known to be hardy in that area and will grow in the right kind of soils, what function does the soil serve and how does one go about "improving" it or adding to its general constituents the items necessary for good growth? To answer this, one should know that the soil is usually considered to be broken-down weathered rocks combined with decayed vegetative plant materials in which are living a myriad of microscopic organisms. Without these, it might be impossible to grow anything at all. Oxygen and water from the air filter down through these soil particles, dissolve chemical compounds as they do so, and aid in supporting the life of the soil organisms as well as the plants. Only when you know the composition of your soil, can you know what fertilizer to add effectively.

Soil Acidity

In addition to the nitrogen, phosphorus, and potash in the soil considered essential to growth, there are also calcium and magnesium, both of which are sometimes deficient. When there is not much calcium in the soil, it is "acid" in reaction; when calcium is prevalent in large quantities it is "alkaline" in reaction. The symbol of pH is used to designate the acidity or alkalinity of the soil, neutral soil having a pH of 7.0; below this figure the pH becomes increasingly acid, to pH 3.5, which is extremely acid. Soils become alkaline above pH 7.0 up to about pH 8.5 or more, which is very alkaline. Actually, the pH scale runs from 1 to 14.

As every experienced gardener knows, soils vary in different parts of the country. In New England they tend to be acid; in the areas of little rainfall in the Midwest they are alkaline, sometimes extremely so; in parts of the East and the West, they are both alkaline and acid. Hence a soil may be strongly acid or alkaline and unsuitable for the growth of certain types of plants. This is where soil testing aids the homeowner. Most state experiment stations have a soil-testing laboratory where small soil samples may be sent in for testing of the acidity. Usually recommendations are made, when the report is returned, of just what should be added to that soil to make it a proper medium for growing plants.

Most plants will grow best in a soil with a pH between 6.5 and 7.0, but apparently trees and shrubs are more versatile. In the Arnold Arboretum the soil tests about pH 5.5 and the majority of the woody plants do well. However, the so-called "acid-soil" plants, like azaleas, rhododendrons, and blueberries, will also grow well on soils even more acid.

To correct for soil pH variations, one adds lime to make the soil more alkaline, or aluminum sulfate (or powdered sulfur, which eventually forms sulfuric acid) to make the soil more acid. The amount depends on how much of a change is desired.

SOIL pH	APPROXIMATE AMOUNT OF GROUND LIMESTONE NEEDED PER 100 SQUARE FEET TO BRING SOIL UP TO A pH OF 6.5
Slightly acid (6.5–6.0)	10 pounds
Medium acid (6.0–5.5)	15 pounds
Strongly acid (5.5–5.0)	20 pounds
Very strongly acid (5.0 and less)	25 pounds

It is advisable to use ground limestone—sometimes ground dolomitic limestone where it is available, because this will have a trace of magnesium in it which may be deficient in some soils.

In order to make the soil more acid, aluminum sulfate can be used at the following suggested rates:

ACIDITY OF SOIL USED AT START	ALUMINUM SULFATE PER 100 SQUARE FEET
Medium acid (pH 5.5 to pH 6.0)	2¾ pounds
Slightly acid (pH 6.5 to pH 7.0)	5½ pounds
Neutral to strongly alkaline (pH 7.0 to pH 8.0)	8¼ pounds

Also, flowers of sulfur can be used to make the soil more acid. This material is cheap and easily available, but it takes much longer to be effective than aluminum sulfate does. In any event, when flowers of sulfur is used it might best be applied in summer, worked into the soil at once, and watered in heavily. It has been suggested that it be applied at 1 to 1½ pounds per 100 square feet for each half pH the soil is to be lowered. Since it is slow in becoming effective, one should be cautious about not adding too much. It might be best to apply it conservatively and test the soil again in several months rather than to use a very large amount all at once.

The first step having been taken, and the soil acidity checked and corrected where necessary, one then considers the matter of fertilizers. If they are to be added, and if the growth of existing plants is not what it should be and an increase is desired, the next steps follow in sequence.

Kinds of Fertilizer

There are many types available on the market: some are sold under specialized trade names; some are special mixtures for acid-soil plants like the azaleas and rhododendrons; and of course there are the various types of manures. It is not our purpose to discuss this subject in detail, since the experienced gardener will know what is best for his needs. For the inexperienced gardener the easiest thing is to obtain one type of fertilizer and try to adapt it for his various garden needs.

Fertilizers under trade name usually come in bags with directions for applications. Many commercial mixtures, such as those used in large amounts on farm land, do not come with directions but merely as marked mixtures with the exact ingredients listed on the outside of the bag as is required by law.

If a 10–10–10 is to be used, it will be applied at one-half the rate of a 5–10–5, for the former has twice as much nitrogen as the latter. If one buys sodium nitrate for instance, it is an extremely powerful fertilizer, and one should have experience with the very small amounts that should be used. There are others in this category also. It is easiest to settle on a fertilizer of a standard mixture, like 5–10–5, at least in the first few years of gardening experience.

Another important thing to determine at the start is the amount of fertilizer one is using. Guessing at amounts often results in either no aid to the plants or in injury from overapplication. Measuring fertilizer is easier than weighing each amount used. It has been determined that such common garden fertilizers as a 5–10–5 or 6–10–4, superphosphate, or some others can be considered to measure out to one pint equaling about one pound. Other calculations may be necessary for other fertilizers, but this is certainly the easiest method to determine exactly the amount of fertilizer one is working with.

Method of Application

The method of applying the fertilizer may have to be varied, depending on the type of plant material. Undoubtedly, broadcasting by hand is the easiest, and a little experimentation is all that is needed to learn how to do this evenly. Applying fertilizers irregularly will quickly show up in alternate streaks of vigorous and poor growth on the lawn, and leaving small piles of fertilizer that should have been broadcast evenly is the quickest way to cause plant injury.

Sometimes, as may be the case in the vegetable garden or around specimen plants, the fertilizer is wanted only for certan plants and not for the whole area; hence it can be applied in bands or circles about such plants, care being taken to apply it evenly over the wide surface where the roots are. Care must also be taken not to leave it on the foliage of valued plants. This will result in the injury or death of the leaves.

Because of this type of injury, which is often hard

to avoid, commercial fertilizers should be applied shortly before a rain or else watered in with a hose immediately after application.

In the long rows of plants in the vegetable garden the fertilizer can be applied as a side dressing merely by distributing it along the sides of the rows. It is often a good idea, if burning the young foliage is to be avoided, to make two light applications of fertilizer two weeks apart rather than one very heavy application. This is easily done by determining the amount to be used and applying half of it to one side of the row at a time.

As mentioned previously, fertilizers can be applied by means of cartridges attached to the garden hose, and when this method is used care should be taken to apply the fertilizer evenly, as called for by the manufacturers of the fertilizer cartridges.

When plants are under irrigation, as in the Far West, fertilizers are frequently applied in the irrigation water itself, calling for a careful study of amounts of fertilizer to use and the even distribution of the water.

The method frequently advocated for applying fertilizers to trees by means of holes punched or bored in the soil is most easily accomplished with machines. Using a crowbar is not easy work and will not appeal to the gardener who is in a hurry. He can either pay to have experts apply the fertilizers to his trees by the punched-hole method—sometimes it is actually blown into the soil by compressed air—or he can take the easy way out and apply it broadcast. The only difficulty (if it is considered such) with the broadcast method of tree fertilizing is that sometimes the tree is growing in a beautiful lawn and the grass may be burned by heavy application.

This is not always a serious obstacle, for the grass will usually grow back quickly, especially if the fertilizer is well watered in immediately. Another way to circumvent burning is to divide the amount into two or three applications, about a week or two apart, each one to be thoroughly watered in. This method is simple, easy, and takes little time.

Finally, we read much now about foliar fertilizer applications—fertilizers in solution sprayed on the foliage. This may have merit in some instances, but it takes equipment and certainly is not a time-saver to the gardener, for many applications have to be made to equal the effects of one soil application.

When to Apply Fertilizers

Fertilizers should be applied early in the growing season. After all, it does take time for the material, when applied broadcast to the surface of the soil, to be dissolved by water, taken down into the soil, translocated to the leaves of the plant, and used in the formation of increased growth, flower, or fruit production. The time the fertilizer is applied will vary, too, with the kind of plant.

Deciduous trees and shrubs should be fertilized early in the spring, just before growth starts. This gives these plants a long growing season to utilize the fertilizers to best advantage. In most areas, they can also be fertilized any time after early mid-September, the objective being to make the fertilizers available to the plant roots until the ground freezes, when the roots are no longer active. This is usually for a long time after the leaves have dropped from the plants. It is obvious that fertilizing in midwinter has little value in areas where the ground freezes.

Deciduous trees and shrubs should not be fertilized between early summer and fall, for fertilizing at this time may stimulate late vegetative growth that will not have a sufficient period to mature properly by the time the leaves fall in the autumn, and such a condition will result in winter injury to those plants.

Evergreens may best be fertilized only in the early spring, just before the growth has started. Although some plantsmen may do it in the fall, this is not a healthy practice generally.

How Much Fertilizer to Apply

Trees: The first year a small tree is planted, it may need an application of fertilizer. If this be the case, one pound of a 5–10–5 or a 6–10–4 could be applied broadcast around the base for each inch in diameter of trunk. If the tree is small, this is applied in a band several feet wide starting 6 to 8 inches from the trunk.

The rates for established deciduous trees for the same types of commercial fertilizer are 2 to 4 pounds per inch in diameter (half that amount for a 10–10–10, which of course has twice as much nitrogen), slightly less for evergreens. The area fertilized is from a line on the ground at the perimeter of the branches and two-thirds of the way toward the trunk.

Shrubs: The amount of fertilizer applied depends on the size of the shrub. For small evergreen shrubs, 2 to 4 pounds of a 5–10–5 per 100 square feet is probably satisfactory. We use this type of fertilizer at the Arnold Arboretum, and have a standard practice of applying from 3½ pounds up to as much as 18 pounds of 5–10–5 per shrub, the larger amounts being for shrubs 15 feet or more tall and as much across.

It is imperative that acid-soil plants like azaleas, rhododendrons, blueberries, and the like have acid soil of about pH 4.5 to 5.5 in which to grow. Help in maintaining this is supplied with the use of acid mulches like peat moss and pine needles. Mulches of maple and elm leaves do not have an acid reaction. Acid-soil plants in the foundation planting around a brick or stucco house may eventually suffer because, over a period of time, the splashing rain will dissolve a certain amount of lime in the mortar which may raise the soil acidity to neutral or alkaline conditions.

Occasionally limestone may be needed around azaleas and rhododendrons in which the pH has gone as low as pH 3. If this is the case, then 40 to 50 pounds of ground limestone might be added per 1,000 square feet so that the pH will be raised nearer to 4.5; then the plants will be able to obtain proper amounts of nitrogen and iron. If the soil is only slightly less acid, but still under pH 4.5, then add only half the above-mentioned amount to bring the soil nearer a pH of 4.5.

Flower Garden: Since many kinds of plants tend to make up the flower garden, it is difficult to give a specific fertilizer recommendation that is perfectly adjusted to all plants. However, using the 5–10–5 or the 6–10–4 as examples, probably 2 to 3 pounds per 100 square feet would be the amounts to try. For special plants in the flower bed the fertilizer should be applied in bands several inches wide on the soil, ringing the base of each plant.

Bulbs will respond to these fertilizers if applied at the same rate as flowers in general. Sometimes this amount is split three ways, one-third applied at time of planting, one-third when the first growth comes out of the ground, and one-third at time of flowering.

Vegetable Garden: Soil reaction is important to vegetables. For instance, we could never grow beets in our garden, could not even get them to germinate, until we learned that they require an almost neutral soil (together with asparagus, cauliflower, celery, lettuce, muskmelon, and spinach). To our acid soil we applied a special application of ground limestone to the row where beets were to be seeded, and following this practice we have had beets every year.

Organic matter is important, too, and can be applied when the garden is plowed each spring. Commercial fertilizers (5–10–5) at the rate of 3 to 5 pounds per 100 square feet, or better still at rates recommended by the local state experiment station, are about right. The smaller amount would be on heavy fertile soils and the larger amounts on light soils. In the vegetable garden the broadcast method (or the side-dressing method) is easiest on the plants, and safest.

MULCHING

A mulch is any material that can be applied to the soil surface without injuring the plants, which reduces water loss from the soil and prevents weed growth. To be practical, it should be inexpensive, easily obtained, and easy to use—although it is difficult to find materials that fulfill all three qualifications completely. Gardeners who have taken the initial time, trouble, and expense to experiment with the best mulch for their garden, find that not only is garden labor materially reduced, but that the mulches are actually beneficial to the growth of their plants.

The first advantage of using mulches is that one has to water less. Mulches reduce the amount of water lost from the soil, cutting down on the amount of watering needed both in short dry spells, and in periods of extended summer droughts.

Another important function of certain mulches is to lower the temperature of the surface soil during extremely hot weather. Soil studies with accurate temperature recordings have proved that under a two-inch mulch of sawdust, for instance, the surface of the soil may be as much as 30° cooler when air temperatures are over 100°F. This means the plant roots have a more uniform temperature in which to grow. Conversely, soil temperatures under mulches in the cold nights of early fall are raised, thus allowing the plants to grow better during this difficult period. This becomes increasingly important in the late fall and early winter, for many mulches prevent the daily freezing and thawing of the surface soil that can result in the heaving of small plants and the breaking of many of their fine feeding rootlets. The roots of plants will continue to grow in soil as long as soil moisture is available. When the soil water freezes, and hence is unavailable to the roots, they stop their growth. Hence it is obvious that a winter mulch aids in the longer growth of roots during this trying period. In the spring the reverse is true; a mulch prevents the soil from thawing out prematurely on the warm days that are followed by night temperatures that drop to well below freezing, thus preventing roots from beginning growth too soon.

For the busy gardener, however, the most obvious advantage of using a mulch is that it prevents weeds from growing—how effectively, depends on the depth and type of mulch used. There will always be certain vigorous weeds that will grow through peat moss or pine needles, for instance, but these can easily be pulled by hand. Black polyethylene film, on the other hand, prevents all weeds from growing.

Some mulching materials add substantial nutrients to the soil after they have begun to disintegrate, thus making them excellent soil amendments. A note of warning must be sounded here, however; nitrifying bacteria are much more active under a mulch, more so under some than others. This means that for the first year or so these bacteria are using up the nitrates already present in the soil at a great rate and many mulches, like sawdust, should never be applied without fertilizing heavily before putting down the mulch to make up for this initial loss. If this is not done, plants may appear yellowish and stunted during the first year of growth, which is probably the reason why many gardeners, after only one trial, have given up mulching as detrimental. However, after the first year or so, the nitrates under a mulch are greatly increased because of the dying soil bacteria, and the plants have a much better medium in which to grow. In general, in fact, mulching aids the tilth (soil texture) and this, too, is a result to be sought by all those growing plants. There are some gardeners who keep a continual mulch on their gardens at all times. One elderly lady has had a hay mulch on her garden for fourteen years, and reports the results have been excellent in every way.

Undoubtedly, then, mulching is an important aid to low maintenance gardening, as long as the right type of mulch is used for the soil and the plants being grown. The gardener, should, however, be aware of some of the dangers of incorrect mulching.

In the first place, a good mulch should not prevent air from getting to the roots of the plants that need it. Many plants, like azaleas and rhododendrons, have most of their feeding roots in the upper few inches of soil. These need moisture, of course, but they also need a certain amount of air. If a heavy mulch of sawdust were applied to a depth of six to eight inches and allowed to pack down hard, or if maple leaves were allowed to pack down, the plants would suffer from lack of air. A light application of sawdust, or a few inches of oak leaves (which do not pack down so hard as those of maple) would be an effective mulch.

Mulches, too, have different reactions when breaking down in the soil. Peat moss, pine peedles, and oak leaves may leave an acid reaction in the soil—to be desired when growing acid-soil plants like azaleas and rhododendrons, but not for all plants. Other materials, like elm and maple leaves, tend to make the soil slightly alkaline.

Mulches are excellent places for disease spores to winter over in and multiply. Because they can also harbor insects and rodents, if serious infestations of any of these pests occur, one of the first control measures is to remove and burn the mulching material. In a reasonably "clean" garden, however, one in which pests are not allowed to gain much headway without strong control measures being taken, it is usually not the mulch that is seriously at fault.

How should you go about choosing the best mulch for your garden? It is impossible to recommend two or three "best" mulches from the many available; the location, weather conditions in the area, cost, and results to be accomplished will all have to be considered. At the Arnold Arboretum in Boston, Massachusetts, for instance, we have tried many things, changing from year to year depending on the availability of mulching material. None have proved harmful to the trees and shrubs; all have proved beneficial.

Cost has been a primary consideration, as it is for most people, and cost is usually closely associated with availability. If one were mulching plants in the great corn-growing areas of the central United States, one would hardly consider using a seaweed mulch, since ground corncobs would be easily available. In areas where local peat is available, one would not go to the expense of shipping in spent hops or cocoa shells. Other factors that should be considered are: how well will the mulch withstand fire; will it scatter in the wind; what will it look like when it is in place? The best plan is to investigate the cheapest type of mulching material available locally, and to use what will do the job best.

APPEARANCE

Because every planting, whether in a public park or home garden, should be neat, a mulching material should be selected that, once applied, remains in a neat condition regardless of high winds, heavy rains, or disturbance by birds or animals. For instance, a mulch of spent hops should remain in a neat condition, but at the Arnold Arboretum there are frequently large flocks of pigeons that find some food material in the hops and continually pick them over and spread them about. Some gardeners like buckwheat hulls, claiming that they make a neat appearance in any garden and so are worth using.

WATER-RETAINING CAPACITY

This is an important point, since a natural mulch retains water. A mulch may also be of some material, like alumnium foil, or polyethylene film, that prevents water from evaporating from the soil but retains no water itself. Of course some, like peat moss and ground corn-cobs, will do both.

EASE OF APPLICATION

In pine-growing areas, pine needles are frequently used, as they are in our own garden. There are many white pines on the place, and each year we have a family project of raking up a sufficient number of the needles in the fall, when they drop from the trees, and applying them to the garden. They cost nothing, are very easily applied, and are about as serviceable as any other mulch we can obtain. They certainly are more easily applied

61

in the diversified perennial border than mulching paper could be.

LENGTH OF TIME SERVICEABLE

It may not always be feasible or advisable to apply the same mulch (that is, pine needles, sawdust, oak leaves) year after year to the same bed. One good mulching may last for several years, and the length of time the material can be expected to perform its duty is important. Theoretically, a mulch of aluminum foil between straight beds of plants or about single trees or shrubs may be expected to last for many years; actually, the wind may rip it loose, vandals may take it, or dogs and small children may dislodge it in short order. Hence a material should be chosen that can be expected to last for several years under expected local conditions.

SUITABILITY

It is seldom advisable to apply a mulch of maple leaves to a bed of rhododendrons and azaleas because maple leaves tend to pack tightly into a thick cover, thus preventing needed air and moisture from circulating easily among the roots. Also, maple leaves can leave an alkaline reaction in the soil, detrimental, in the long run, to plants like rhododendrons and azaleas which prefer acid soil.

Another example would be the use of buckwheat hulls about small succulents that grow flat on the ground. Being black, the buckwheat hulls may absorb sufficient heat on hot summer days to injure those parts of the leaves coming in contact with them. It might be far better in this case to use crushed gray stone.

FIRE HAZARD

In public places there is always the possibility that someone may set fire to a very dry mulch. Peat moss can become powder dry in the hot summer. If a lighted cigarette stub is thrown on such material, especially in a high wind, fire will quickly result and can be extremely difficult to put out. In many home plantings the fire hazard is not an important one.

DEPTH AND TIME OF APPLICATION

In applying any mulch, one must keep in mind the fact that the roots of plants need a certain amount of pure air, as do the leaves. When soils are wet and then are so thoroughly tamped that, as they dry out, they compact into a bricklike substance without air spaces between the soil particles. This results in death or injury to the plants, merely because of lack of air to the roots.

A mulch must allow water to seep through it to the soil beneath, as well as a small amount of pure air. Some mulching materials (for instance, paper pulp) cake when they are dry, thus reducing the amount of air allowed through. Others, like coffee grounds, are so fine that if a deep mulch is applied (5 to 6 inches) little air may reach the soil below, and hence the mulch would do more harm than good when applied so thickly. Dried oak leaves, on the other hand, might be applied 5 inches thick. It really depends on the kind of material used. There are no definite rules for the exact thickness of all mulches, since even the soil itself varies, although a thicker mulch might be applied to a sandy or gravelly soil, for example, than would be necessary on a heavy clay soil. In general, however, it might be said that 2 to 3 inches of mulching material is satisfactory in many cases.

Actually, experience is the best teacher as to the

depth of mulches. They should be deep enough to kill the weeds and prevent the soil from drying out, but not so deep that they prevent pure air from reaching the surface soil.

In placing a very wet mulch like spent hops direct from the brewery on extremely hot days, one should be certain that the materials do not touch the plant stems. Being thoroughly wet, when the temperature is well above 90°F., such mulches tend to absorb heat to such an extent that they can actually kill the plant parts with which they come in contact. In applying spent hops a few years ago, we found a lilac with stems two inches in diameter at the base that had been quickly killed merely because the hops had been piled around the base of the plant on a very hot day. In applications of this nature, be certain that the mulching materials do not come within a foot or more of the stems of the plant, and thus avoid serious injury.

Some materials can harbor rodents. For instance, last summer we were using black polyethylene film as a material around the base of Oriental Crab Apples to kill quack grass. The film was brought right up to the trunk of the trees. It killed the quack grass, but in late fall it was noticed that field mice were starting to hibernate under the film. Fortunately, plenty of food was available for them until that time; but in the winter, when food becomes unavailable to them, "protecting" their runs and nests in this fashion by the use of polyethylene film is practically ensuring mouse injury to the young tree trunks. In order to prevent this, the film was removed and poison grain placed about each tree as necessary insurance against injury.

Mulching materials can be applied at any time when available. To do the most good they should be applied well before summer droughts and before the time weed growth starts actively. Also, to do the most good as a winter protection, mulches should be applied well before the time the ground freezes in the fall.

Mulching Materials

The following is a list of some of the mulching materials that have been used or are available in various parts of the country. Some are better than others; but in many situations where poor soil and summer drought combine to make growth poor, any one of these materials used as a mulch should result in better plant growth than when no mulch at all is used.

Bark: Some large lumber companies grind up the bark of certain trees, making this material available for mulching purposes. So, in certain areas of the country it is possible to obtain redwood bark, pine bark, yellow birch bark, and others. Some even go so far as to grind the materials into particles of different diameters so that one may obtain an "all-purpose," "fine grit," "pea," or "chestnut" size. Obviously these would have merit for different purposes and might well be experimented with in areas where they are economically available.

Buckwheat Hulls: A good mulch where available economically, buckwheat hulls do not pack down like leaves, but remain light and well aerated, not absorbing much water themselves, and so allowing small amounts to trickle down to the soil underneath. They are black, and take two years or more to decompose. They are best applied 1 to 2 inches in depth, a 50-pound bag covering approximately 65 square feet to a depth of one inch. Apparently weed seeds do not seem to germinate in them, but, as in other mulches, weeds can grow through them from the soil beneath. These may be spindly, and are easily pulled, if done in time.

Winds do not seem to blow buckwheat hulls, and if a water wand is used when watering, the water can easily be placed beneath the mulch. When applied this way, the entire mulch seems to raise up a bit as the water spreads over the soil, the mulch returning to its proper place after the water has soaked into the ground. With this type of watering (without pressure), and the ability of buckwheat hulls to reduce soil water loss markedly, it is unnecessary to water plants under such a mulch more than every 10 to 14 days, even in the severest of summer droughts.

Cocoa Shells: These are the shells from the cocoa bean, and have been used as soil amendments for several years. As received direct from the cocoa- or chocolate-producing plants, they are very dry, light, and easily handled. They retain moisture for long periods, and are rather slimy to walk on after about six months in the open, but the excessive leaching of potassium salts can be injurious to some plants (particularly azaleas and rhododendrons) where the material is used as a very deep mulch.

However, when used judiciously, cocoa shells apparently do little harm and considerable good. They have nearly as much nitrogen as dried chicken manure and more than dried cow manure. When applied as a mulch at a depth of not more than 2 to 3 inches, beneficial results should appear, especially from the comparatively high nitrogen. When worked into the soil, cocoa shells result in the better growth of many kinds of plants, woody and herbaceous alike. Though cocoa shells may not be the perfect mulch, they bear serious consideration if they can be obtained inexpensively, for with their high content of nitrogen, phosphoric acid, and potash (N P K) they serve the dual purpose of fertilizer and mulch.

Coffee Grounds: When coffee beans were bought at the grocery store and ground at home, it was an old-fashioned custom to place coffee grounds about garden plants and house plants, and the results were said to be excellent. Today, with instant coffee, coffee grounds are available only from the few factories processing coffee beans. Because these coffee grounds are very fine, they cake readily when exposed to the weather. This prevents normal amounts of pure air from reaching the plant roots. As a result, coffee grounds should not be used as a heavy mulch but always as a light mulch an inch or so in depth. It is doubtful if they are as beneficial to the soil as are some of the other mulching materials.

Corncobs (ground):   Often a very cheap item in rural areas, it has several advantages as a mulch when applied 2 to 3 inches deep. However, because it has been found that when corn and cobs are ground together they can be fed to steers and hogs in the form of mash, this material may become scarce for mulching purposes.

Grass Clippings: Clippings from the lawn are sometimes so thick that they must be raked off. These can be used as a mulch, but if applied too green and too deep they heat up considerably, and become a dense mat through which the proper amount of air and water fail to penetrate. They may be put to a better use by being mixed with dried leaves or garden trash in the compost heap so that eventually they reach the garden soil as compost rather than as pure mulch.

Ground Tobacco Stems: In certain southern areas this material can be obtained inexpensively. It is coarse, and has not been entirely satisfactory on rose beds because the diseased leaves can fall down and become lodged in the material, thus providing new infestations of the black-spot disease. However, because it is refuse from the tobacco plant it will undoubtedly aid in the restraining of insect attacks, and so has merit as a mulch in areas where it can be obtained inexpensively.

Leaves: One of the most common of mulching materials, dead leaves are always available wherever trees and shrubs are grown. Because there has been much agitation against burning them, more and more gardeners are being trained to use them either as a winter mulch on the garden or in compost operations. The leaves from some species of trees are often better than those from certain others for mulching materials. Take, for instance, the leaves of the Sugar and Norway Maples, as well as the poplar. These pack flat and tight on the soil surface, thus excluding sufficient air and moisture when applied to any appreciable depth. This type of mulch is particularly harmful to rhododendrons and azaleas, the roots of which are close to the soil surface and need plenty of air and moisture.

On the other hand, oak leaves are ideal for mulching. They do not pack nearly as tightly as those of maple; they seem to retain a fluffy character in the mulch that is conducive to good aeration and allows ample penetration of rain water into the soil.

Some who grind leaves up in a leaf mulcher feel that the results are far superior to merely applying the dead leaves themselves. It is probably true that the cut-up material does not tend to blow as readily as large leaves do, and this may be an advantage in some places.

As noted before, as leaves from some species of plants decompose (notably oaks and pines), they tend to leave an acid reaction, one of the reasons why they are the best kind of mulching material for azaleas and rhododendrons; while those from others (notably elm) may leave an alkaline reaction. It should always be kept in mind that there is little about the garden more combustible than dried leaves and that they will blow away in a high wind. The larger the leaves, the more unsightly the general aspect of the mulch. If these hazards are not serious in the garden, use the leaves as a mulch by all means.

Peanut Shells: These make another good mulch in areas close to the southeastern parts of the United States where peanuts are grown and processed. They are light and easily handled, and some tests in the production of greenhouse tomatoes show that they are well suited for mulching this crop in the greenhouse. In fact, shipping charges were so low (because of the light weight) that they have been sold in Massachusetts and Ohio in recent years for use in growing commercial tomato crops. It is conceivable that if they are not completely free of peanuts, if used outdoors they might prove a great attraction to rodents. Here again, availability and cost are the chief factors in their use. Since they contain .95 percent nitrogen, they do have some fertilizing value.

Peat Moss: The merits of peat moss are well known, and it is probably one of the most widely used mulching materials, although it is certainly not the least expensive. It is impossible to make specific statements about contents, since there are all kinds of peat in use. The least expensive are those that come from the local peat bogs, frequently containing considerable amounts of soil. The most uniform are those that have been processed and come from large deposits in Michigan, Canada, or Europe. The gardener with only a small garden is usually willing to pay premium prices to obtain uniform material of a light brown color that looks well after it has been applied and contains relatively few (if any) weed seeds.

It has merit when mixed with certain types of soils, but woe to the gardener who thinks that because a little amount is good for the soil, a large amount can be better! When completely dry, it takes an extremely long time for a large amount of dry peat to absorb moisture, the reason why young plants planted in almost 100 percent peat may die in a long drought where plants in the normal soil nearby may not. The small amounts of rain in a dry summer fail to soak through a great depth of dry peat, although they may do so in the soil. Mixed with a goodly amount of soil, however, peat moss does not become such a hazard as only peat alone.

Native peats can be bought by the bag, the bushel, or the truckload, while processed peats are usually dried and pressed into bales for easy shipping. Bales are available in different sizes, some containing 4 cubic feet and weighing about 55 pounds, others 6 cubic feet and weighing about 95 pounds, and others 7½ or 8 cubic feet. To estimate the amount of this material needed, a 95-pound bale of pressed peat, broken up and well moistened, will cover approximately 300 square feet of soil surface in a layer one inch thick.

Some peats have 98 percent organic matter and have been advertised as "lasting in soil service up to ten years." This is probably an optimistic estimate, but it shows that they cannot be expected to break down very soon. They have been estimated to hold anywhere from 600 to 1200 percent water when compared on a dry-weight basis, so their water-absorbing qualities are high indeed. But, as noted above, completely dry peat absorbs water very slowly, so that it is best to moisten peat well before it is applied to dry soil. It is usually acid in reaction, 3.6 to 6.8 pH being the normal range.

It is suggested that peat-moss mulches be applied from 1 to 3 inches deep, depending on the reason for using the mulch. The deeper mulch would of course tend to keep more weeds from growing, although even at the three-inch depth there will be some that eventually have to be pulled out after a period. During winter, when used as a protective mulch, an even deeper application of up to four inches might well be in order.

Pine Needles: A great part of the gardening public lives in areas where pine needles are available, and these make excellent and often very inexpensive mulching materials, especially in areas where they may be had merely for the raking and hauling. They are acid in reaction and hence ideal for use on acid-loving plants like azaleas and rhododendrons. The particular gardener will note that there is a difference in quality of mulch made by needles from the different species of pine. White Pine, for instance, has soft flexible needles that make a very fine mulch, while those of Red Pine are more coarse and may not deteriorate for three or four years. White Pine needles could be used in mulching the smaller plants and Red Pine in mulching the shrubs and the trees.

In general, pine needles do not absorb much moisture themselves, but let the rain quickly filter down through to the soil, one of the reasons why they are so good for the surface-rooted azaleas and rhododendrons that need air as well as moisture about their roots. Weed seeds also will have a difficult time germinating in a pine mulch, especially during dry weather when the mulch dries out.

Another advantage of the pine needles is the fact that they can be easily lifted with rake or fork. If weeds do grow through, as they will, a prompt lifting of the mulch with a pitchfork, and then laying the needles down again in the same place but covering the weeds growing from the soil, can aid materially in discouraging them from too much growth.

Still another advantage is the fact that these mulches can be easily raked off in the spring, if desired, piled, and then used later where needed. We have been using a White Pine mulch at the same place in the garden, renewed every other year or so, for as much as eight years, with excellent results. Commercial fertilizers applied to the mulch surface are quickly washed into the soil by rain or water from the hose, and so they are not held in the mulch to encourage root growth above the soil level. If the soil becomes too acid because pine needles are used continuously on the garden, sufficient lime can easily be applied and washed through the needles to the soil, bringing the soil pH up to the desired level. Needless to say, this also is an excellent qualification for pine mulches in the garden.

If applied three or four inches deep, pine needles act as a splendid insulation on the soil against high temperatures in the summer. This, combined with the crisscross effect of the needles, resulting in good soil aeration, makes pine needles one of the best of mulching materials.

Polyethylene Film: Science has provided horticulture with this excellent material that can be used for all kinds of purposes in storing, shipping, and propagating plants. Its value stems from the fact that gases like nitrogen, carbon dioxide, oxygen, and others can pass through it without much difficulty, but water and water vapor cannot. The clear film is of no value as a mulch, merely because sunlight passes readily through it, and weeds grow almost as well underneath it as they do in the open soil.

However, black polyethylene has all the properties of the clear plastic except for the fact that it excludes the light. Used as a mulch it has possibilities, but also one great drawback—it will hold the moisture in the soil, but it will not let water into the soil unless special steps, which will be described later, are taken. Experiments show that this mulching material if handled properly will last as a mulch for many years. It comes in several thicknesses, but for mulching purposes a thickness of .015 inches is probably satisfactory.

Normally, water travels by capillarity in the soil, both up and down and sidewise, but the movement from side to side is very slow. Consequently, in very dry periods, with a large area covered by this film, it is understandable that the soil can be deficient of moisture underneath it, no matter how often water is applied from sprinkler or hose. This difficulty can be overcome simply, in either of two ways: If hose watering is desired, merely see to it that the hose is held for a considerable length of time at the base of the plant where it comes through the film, thus allowing water to spread around underneath the film and to all parts of the area, eventually soaking down into the soil. The chief difficulty with this method is that it creates special work and the technique can easily be faulty, that is, not enough water or not often enough.

By far the simplest method is to use an ice pick or screwdriver to poke holes in the film after it is in place on the ground, especially in the lower spots to which the water drains. If the holes are at about six-inch intervals, possibly closer in the depressions, sufficient water will be allowed through to keep the soil moist in all but the driest of summers. For prized, newly planted specimens, a combination of these two practices, together with checking on the soil under the polyethylene during the dry periods, will suffice.

Another advantage in using the polyethylene film is that it will quickly kill the grass over which it is placed. Grass is always an important competitor of the newly planted tree or shrub for soil moisture and nutrients. At the end of the summer, or in the fall if need be, the plastic film can be lifted and stored for use again the next year, but this only creates work and it is far more satisfactory to leave it around the plant permanently.

Salt Hay, Hay, Straw: These three materials have always been used for mulching, especially with agricultural crops and fruits, but to be effective they should be 8 to 10 inches deep. They are still used to some extent in the garden, but their chief difficulties are that they are bulky, often unkempt, and can bring into the garden a large amount of weed seeds. Also, they can harbor mice. For winter use as protecting materials they still have their place, but in most gardens, especially the small, well-kept ones, other neater mulching materials are usually used. However, in mulching fruit trees and small fruits there is nothing better or more economical. Many experiments over the years have definitely proved that, after the first three years, nitrates are considerably higher under the hay mulch; soil moisture is raised; growth is better; and yield is better than those of trees grown under cultivation. The rodent hazard must be met forthrightly, and a vigorous program of placing wire mesh about the base of the tree trunks and placing poison grain about the trees to combat the mice should yield favorable results. In other words, heavy hay mulching is a satisfactory system of orchard management, the chief regulating factor being the cost of application.

Sawdust: At many lumber mills about the country sawdust can be obtained at very little cost, and these sources of cheap mulching material should not be overlooked. The type of tree from which the sawdust comes makes little difference in the long run, whether it is pine, oak, maple, or birch. As a mulch, applied at a depth of about two inches, it will aid markedly in reducing weed growth, in preventing water evaporation from the soil, and in reducing soil temperatures during the hot summer months.

Many studies have been made with various kinds of sawdust. The most important fact to keep in mind is that for the good of the plants a generous application of a complete fertilizer should be made to the soil before the sawdust is applied.

There is always a reduced amount of available nitrogen in the soil under sawdust, especially the first year after application. This has been clearly noted in many experiments, resulting in reduced growth of plants when compared with those having no mulch. This is also true with other mulching materials, but especially with sawdust. The defect can be offset with the application of fertilizer *before* mulching. If applied after the sawdust is in place, the nutrients may be held in the sawdust and hence may be unavailable to the plant roots for a long period.

Experiments with mulching commercial blueberry plantings have proved that a two-inch sawdust mulch (if preceded by an application of fertilizer) increases yield over a three-year period. No great differences were found between hardwood and softwood sawdust, except that the latter does not tend to break down so quickly. Nor are there any harmful effects (to the plants) from the resins in the softwood sawdust.

After several years, when the sawdust has deteriorated, it can be worked into the soil as a means of "soil improvement." However, in the heavily planted perennial garden where soil digging is not advisable, merely applying more sawdust is all that is necessary. As it breaks down and becomes humus, it serves its purpose in the surface soil, and more applied on top—if not too deep—fulfills the purpose of a continual mulch.

Spent Hops: Spent hops have proved quite successful. The Arnold Arboretum has been fortunate in being
comparatively near two breweries having an ample supply of spent hops to dispose of and can obtain them
merely by hauling at regular intervals. These hops had
the following analysis:

Water	87.67%
Nitrogen	.40
Organic matter	11.49
Ash	.49
pH	4.8

This material was used for over ten years. There are
several drawbacks, for it is obvious that since they are
obtained from a brewery they have an extremely high
water content. (For every 238 pounds of dry material,
we were hauling 1,740 pounds of water.) They also
have an objectionable odor which is noticeable on a
warm day but disappears in about two weeks after application. Third, spent hops attract pigeons and rodents.

The merits of spent hops far outweigh their disad-
vantages when used as a mulch. Because they are wet
when first applied, they do not blow away on a windy
day. And, what is more important, even when dry (after
weeks of drought) these hops will not burn appreciably.
Time and again it has been noticed that plants mulched
with spent hops have not been injured by surrounding
grass fires. The fire has burned up to the edge of the
mulch, and stopped. Because of this, we have actually
used spent hops for mulching as a fire preventive.

Although slightly more acid than our soil, the spent-
hops mulch has been applied to practically all the kinds
of trees and shrubs in the Arboretum except a dozen of
the outstanding lime-requiring plants. We have seen no
ill effects from their use except when applied on days

preceding high temperatures and when the hops are heaped around the base of a small tree trunk or shrub with numerous stems. When this occurs and the temperatures are high, the material does heat noticeably and can kill stems several inches in diameter. Hence, the only precaution to be taken in applying this material is to keep it a foot or so away from the basal stems of trees and shrubs.

The spent-hops mulch is applied 4 to 6 inches thick and lasts about two years before disintegrating appreciably. Quack grass and other vigorous weeds will eventually grow through it, but this mulch is ideal for conserving soil water and has necessarily been applied at all seasons of the year without injury to plants.

Sugar Cane: This material has been offered by some of the sugar mills in the South after the cane stalks have been pressed and subjected to very high temperatures. Usually it is ground—it has a pH value of from 4.5 to 5.2, has a water-holding capacity of over 340 percent, and supposedly decomposes into almost pure humus. Recommendations for a mulch suggest that it be applied about two inches thick on the soil surface. This is another mulching material for extensive use in areas in the sugar-producing parts of the country.

Wood Chips, Wood Shavings: With the advent of brush-chipping machines, wood chips have become a very important mulching material, especially in large parks and arboretums where there is always pruning work being done. They are applied usually about 2 to 3 inches deep, but here, as with sawdust, it is advisable to give the soil an ample application of high-nitrogen fertilizer or complete fertilizer before the chips are applied. They last at least two years, sometimes longer, birch chips of course disintegrating before pine and oak chips.

They are coarse, allowing for the easy wetting of the soil from light rains. They do not burn readily, will not blow (like much lighter shavings), and go a long way in conserving soil moisture. At the same time, because they are coarse they allow good soil aeration. They should be used wherever available, but because they are heavy, shipping costs are too high to make it economically feasible to ship them any great distances. If a local supply is available, the chances are that it will pay to use this material as a mulch. We have found coarse wood chips lasting (as a mulch on the ground) at least three years. It is unwise to use elm wood in the making of the chips since such material could conceivably aid in spreading the Dutch Elm disease.

Wood shavings burn more readily and are blown by high winds more easily than wood chips, but if neither of these drawbacks proves serious then they too can be used as mulching material.

These are only some of the mulching materials available. Others occasionally used are aluminum foil, sprayed asphalt, cranberry vines, fiber glass, gravel or crushed stone, walnut shells, roofing papers, seaweed, and ground banana stalks. It should be pointed out, however, that it might be inadvisable to use new or untried materials for mulching purposes until they have been tried or assessed by some of the state agricultural experiment stations. In general, materials that conserve soil moisture and at the same time allow sufficient soil aeration prove satisfactory, for these act as valued time savers in weed control for the busy gardener. If, later, they decompose and add essential chemicals to the soil, so much the better, for then they serve the dual purpose of mulch and fertilizer as well.

HERBICIDES

Chemical weed killers should head every list of labor-saving devices for the gardener. Now no one need kneel on the ground, laboriously digging out each weed in the lawn, for there is a chemical spray that with two or three applications will eradicate a major part of the broad-leaved weeds from the lawn. Poison ivy, being one of the most pernicious of woody weeds in eastern gardens and woodlands, can also be killed by chemical sprays. Unwanted saplings or "brush" along the roadside, the woods walk, the stone fence, or under the cross-country power lines has been effectively and cheaply killed for many years now by proper spray procedures. Most stumps can also be effectively killed merely by spraying them with a highly concentrated chemical herbicide of the right kind.

There are so many herbicides being offered and the publicity about them makes weed elimination sound so easy, that the homeowner who makes one application (possibly at the wrong time) is very disappointed if all the weeds are not killed at once. In fact, his first failure may be responsible for his treating all herbicides with great skepticism. They must be properly used at the proper time, and when this is done they can well be among the best labor-savers and money-savers in garden maintenance. In general, chemical herbicides can be divided into three groups: those that are selective in killing only certain types of plant growth; those that kill or at least seriously injure all types of plant growth; and finally those that, when applied to newly cultivated soil, kill the germinating weed seeds.

Selective Herbicides

This is by far the most important group, for here are those that will kill the broad-leaved weeds in the lawn without injuring the grass, or the woody seedlings and brush without injuring the grass. Recently, herbicides have been developed that when applied to certain grasses will kill those grasses without apparently injuring the woody plants close by. Some have been found to be adaptable for use in keeping down the weed population in carrots, strawberries, or asparagus, and most recently we were most pleased to find one that was supposed to be effective in killing the grass in raspberries without injuring the raspberries!

The 2,4-D [2,4-dichlorophenoxy acetic acid] sprays are highly volatile, once applied. They are used chiefly to kill broad-leaved lawn weeds and do not injure grass. They should be applied on a mild day when there is no wind, for their injurious effect to trees and shrubs is now very well known, since severe injury to trees can occur when even a slight drift of wind sends some spray on the foliage. One young arborist, supposing the spray tank filled with material for killing insects, sprayed the trees and shrubs on a property only to be sued shortly thereafter when all the plants started to die. Actually, his tank had been full of 2,4-D weed killer. These materials are so highly toxic to broad-leaved plants that it is always advisable to keep a separate sprayer for this purpose, good protective insurance in using any weed killer, but especially those containing 2,4-D.

When 2,4-D sprays are applied to the lawn, the nozzle should be close to the grass and extreme care should be taken that the spray does not hit shrubs or trees. If, on a windy day, a gust of wind blows the spray into a tree close by, that tree will show severe injury within a few days. In fact, the mere evaporation of heavy doses of this material to herbaceous weeds under trees or shrubs has been known to seriously injure the woody plant parts growing above but not touched with the spray. Extreme caution must be taken, especially in the period of late spring when all growth is lush and succulent, for injury can be expected to certain over-sensitive plants like *Malus ioensis* 'Plena' within fifty feet of where the material has been used, depending on the direction of the wind, even after application. In fact, the odor has lasted about an area for as long as sixty days, so that it is obvious why oversensitive plants may be injured even though they are not touched with the actual spray at spraying time.

There are several methods of applying herbicides to the lawn. They can be mixed with the proper amount of water and then used from a hand-pump sprayer for spot application. Or they can be applied (according to directions that come with the material) in a hand sprayer which is attached to the garden hose. If there are not too many broad-leaved weeds in the lawn, the 2,4-D herbicide can be mixed with the proper amount of water and carried around in a bucket. It is applied by simply using a stick to which a sponge is atttached and dabbing the weeds with the wetted sponge. Finally, there have been three-foot bars of wax manufactured containing 2,4-D and these are merely pulled over the weedy spots in the lawn on a hot sunny day when the temperatures are above 80°F.

In using herbicides one should know that certain ones (2,4-D) are volatile and leave no residue in the soil, but others like "Amazine" (ammonium sulfamate), or "Ammate" and "Simazine" do leave a residue in the soil for varying amounts of time, and the accumulation of this residue over a period of years after repeated applications can result in unexpected injury to various plants. Also, if these are applied on a bank, followed by heavy rainfalls, injury can occur to plants wherever the run-off from that bank occurs—sometimes a hundred feet or more away from the spot where the material was originally applied. So, know the herbicides you choose to use and their residual characteristics, and use them accordingly.

KILLING GRASSES

There are materials on the market that kill certain kinds of grasses without injuring woody plants close by. We have been most interested in this particular problem in the Arnold Arboretum, and probably everyone is who tries to grow plants in an area where Witch Grass thrives. We set out young woody plants on the grounds, digging a sizable hole and of course placing the sod removed in the bottom of the hole to rot and thus afford nutrients for the young plant. However, in a very few months, unless we mulch the plant or hoe about it (which is always expensive) Witch Grass grows in vigorously. It is not long before this is competing for moisture and nutrients with the young plants, and sometimes it can actually kill the young plant that is not properly established. Dalapon sprayed on the grass kills the grass but does not injure the plant.

Crab Grass is always a bad lawn weed, for which there now are effective controls (materials now named "Balax," "Bandane," "Dacthal," DSMA, MSMA, etc.). Annual Bluegrass is controlled with "Betasan." "Silvex" is another material especially effective in controlling buttercup, chickweed, dandelion, Ground Ivy, pennywort, plantain and Poison Ivy, among others. Another chemical currently available under the trade name of "Casoron G4" (a dichlobenil weed and grass killer) at this time of writing is one of the best weed and grass killers around established woody plants. It is a white granulated powder, applied in November after the ground has frozen. We have used the current material at the rate of 1 ounce per 22 square feet and it has killed all the grass and weeds in the nursery row for nearly a full year. Supposedly it is non-cumulative in the soil, but recently there have been instances of its accumulation in the soil after being applied annually for many years in the same plot.

These are just current examples of chemicals available for specific weed-killing jobs, but they must be sought out and used according to directions. Careful compliance with the remarks on the can or package will forestall serious trouble. I remember all too well my experience in first trying out a new Witch-Grass killer. I had been struggling with the Witch Grass about my grapes for years, and welcomed the opportunity of a spray that would eliminate the pest easily. I applied the material at the proper time and in the proper way, but on arriving at the end of the row found I still had half a tank full of spray. Being of a thrifty nature, and anxious to do a thorough job, I went back over the same row with the remainder of the spray. We were very pleased in the next few days when the Witch Grass began to die, but not so satisfied when, six weeks later, the grapes began to die from the material that had been applied at twice its recommended strength!

STUMPS

Stump killing is very simple: merely mix a goodly amount of concentrated "brush killer" (the current rates are 3 pints of a commercial brush killer in 10 gallons of fuel oil, kerosene or discarded crankcase oil) and brush it or spray it generously on the stump in question. Most commonly used brush killers now contain 2,4,5-TP [2-2,4,5-trichlorophenoxy propionic acid]. This can be done at any time of the year, but it is best to do it immediately after the stump has been cut. It is advisable to daub the material on the sides of the trunk left exposed above the ground as well as on the cut surface. It is a simple matter to clean out a few woody seedlings in the garden by merely cutting them down and then with a paintbrush and a can of mixed brush killer daub the stubs generously with this material. They will eventually die. This approach eliminates the necessity of digging out the roots. Also, for a fee, arborists have heavy machines to chip down stumps to inches below the ground line, thus saving the expensive digging out and removal of the whole stump.

PRE-EMERGENCE SPRAYS

Pre-emergence sprays can be applied to the soil, after it has been cleaned of weeds, to prevent the germination of new weed seeds. Some of these are effective for several months and have merit where the woody plants, even though small, are well established. There are many of these chemicals available, some of them harmful to certain woody plants but not to others. As far as the home gardener is concerned, he should approach this group with a completely experimental point of view. At the present time there is no material available that can be sprayed up and down the rows of the newly planted vegetable garden which will kill the germinating weed seeds but which, on the other hand, will allow all the vegetable seeds to germinate and grow properly.

BRUSH KILLERS

The current "brush killers" usually contain a mixture of 2,4-D [2,4-dichlorophenoxy acetic acid] and 2,4, 5-TP [2-2,4,5-trichlorophenoxy propionic acid]. This combination has been found to be more effective in killing woody plants than either chemical alone. These materials are finding wide use in spraying areas along highways, railroad right-of-ways, and the brush beneath power lines. The best time to apply brush killers is while the plants are still in active growth during the late spring, when the leaves are young and succulent. When foliage applications are made in the late summer, the percentage of killing is often not so great.

Brush killers can also be mixed with fuel oil or kerosene and sprayed on the basal parts of woody brush when it is dormant. However, it is essential to cover *all sides* of the stems to get a good killing. Sometimes a good approach is to use the dormant spray in late fall or winter, followed up in late spring with the foliar spray to kill any shoots that have grown in the interim. Such spraying usually gives excellent control.

It might well be that the best time-saver would be to adopt a philosophical attitude toward many weeds. Take, for instance, those in the lawn. The perfectionist wants to rid his lawn of every plant that differs from the kinds of grass he is growing, and is willing to spend hours and hours in so doing. I knew of a small group of dwellings in which there was one such individual who spent all his spare time weeding his lawn while his neighbors were out golfing and doing numerous other things they wanted to do. A cursory examination of the lawns in front of these houses showed the comparative results in a prominent way. Those with poor lawns were continually being urged to follow the excellent example set by the man with the perfect lawn. After several months of trying attempts to do so, the heads of the other households sent a delegation to the enthusiastic weeder to ask him to please cease from attaining such perfection in his lawn so that they could spend their spare time doing other things.

To some, a few dandelions in front of the house is a challenge; to others they are merely a spot of yellow. A little effort with 2,4-D or a digging tool can eliminate most of these weeds, but the gardener who has learned how to live with such things, eradicating the worst if and when there is a little time—but only if and when he chooses—is the one who will get the most pleasure out of life. In the flower garden, and possibly even in the vegetable garden, one can practice weed control more effectively with mulches.

The low-maintenance-minded gardener had best study his specific needs himself and then investigate the weed killers currently available. Using the wrong one, or the right one in the wrong way, could let him in for some decidedly high-maintenance replacement problems!

PESTICIDES

Because of the general interest in air, soil, and water pollution, there are an increasing number of regulations concerning the use of pesticides. The gardener using pesticides should be certain that they are cleared with regard to state and federal laws and, if uncertain, should check with the state Pesticide Board or the local County Agricultural Extension Agent. The right pesticide, applied at the right time, is the quickest way to control or eliminate the pest concerned. It is not necessary to have a whole closet filled with sprays and dusts for specific pests, since some like Malathion, easily control a number of different kinds of pests when applied at the right time. In fact one might well obtain a general purpose mixture, which is usually a wettable powder or dust containing one or more insecticides and fungicides, and is used to control several common pests. New formations and mixtures are continually appearing, some in the form of aerosol cans. A good way to be sure you are using the right pesticide at the right time is to obtain the most recent recommendations from your state agricultural experiment station. Most gardens have similar common-pest problems, and the majority of these can be controlled with easily available pesticides or general pesticide mixtures.

CHEMICALS THAT KILL ALL GROWTH

There are some of these on the market. Their use is usually restricted to the weeds and grass that come up in the roadway or between the bricks on the terrace or in the walk—in places where it does not matter if a poison is retained by the soil. Most of the weed killers already discussed do not leave toxic materials in the soil for any length of time. This group of chemicals may well leave toxic residues in the soil that would not be harmful in gutters or roadways, but certainly would be decidedly harmful in garden soil. There are also other materials like Stoddard's Solvent or Sovasol (a cleaning fluid) which when applied to grass kills only the above-ground portions, not the roots. It will kill foliage of woody plants in a few hours' time, but not the woody stems that send out new leaves later. Its best use is for the control of annual weeds, especially purslane. The best time to spray these fast-growing summer pests is when they are only a quarter-inch high, and Sovasol kills them within a few hours. It is highly volatile and leaves no toxic material in the soil.

There are precautions to be taken with weed killers, as everyone knows who has considered using them. Take as an example the eradication of Poison Ivy. If it is growing in the open field, there are several quickly applied "killer" compounds that prove satisfactory. However, when the Poison Ivy is growing in shrubbery or under trees one must remember the fact that roots of other plants are underneath those of the Poison Ivy or intermingled with them, and a soaking of the soil with a destructive weed killer can damage both types of plants. Even when the foliage is supposed to be merely "slightly moistened" with the weed killer, damage can result to the roots of other plants, as we found out the hard way several years ago when we were first trying out one of the experimental materials.

The plot we selected for trial was in the woods under some fine young pine trees with trunks six inches in diameter. The chemical killed the Poison Ivy all right, even with just a hasty moistening of the foliage, but six weeks later we noticed that the White Pines were severely damaged, and later they died. We repeated the experiment elsewhere with the same results, and so have never again used this material as a weed killer in areas where we want selective killing of only certain types of plants.

Many a gardener will find among the available weed killers some that are selective which he can use for a particular purpose, and they will act as time-savers. One should obtain the latest information on such materials from the nearest state experiment station, where impartial tests are usually conducted. Also, there are always articles covering the uses of new weed killers in horticultural publications.

CHEMICALS TO PREVENT GROWTH

Recently work has been done at several of the state experiment stations with chemicals that are supposed to prevent or retard growth. Wouldn't it be wonderfully convenient to have some soluble chemical that could be sprayed on plant material to "arrest" growth at some particular stage? For instance, let a lawn grow to just the right height and proper degree of luxuriousness, then spray to keep it that way for the remainder of the season.

Such chemical solutions may be forthcoming at some future date. However, those tried up to the present time, chiefly maleic hydrazide and alpha-naphthalene-acetic acid, cannot be used promiscuously on all plants with the same results. Some have "arrested" growth for a period of anywhere from a week to several months. However, the results have varied greatly. Current weather conditions can affect the results materially; in addition, the aftereffects of repeated sprays of the same materials on the same plants or the same area of soil may have injurious effects.

Consequently, as far as short-cutting certain garden operations like pruning or cutting grass, it is inadvisable to depend on the chemicals that have been used experimentally for this purpose up to the present.

Chemicals have been used to control the flowering and fruit set of some kinds of fruit trees; to destroy the blossoms of the fruiting forms of the Ginkgo, Honeylocust, Horse-chestnut and ash so that the objectionable fruits will not be formed. It was found with lilacs, however, that in order to apply the spray at the proper time, the flower blossoms would have to be prematurely injured. Chemicals have also been used to inhibit the sprouting of plants held in storage for lengthy periods. Since work with these materials is still in the experimental stages, one should obtain the latest information from the nearest agricultural experiment station before attempting to use them. Application must be made at certain definite strengths and at specific times for specific plants if desired results are to be obtained, or actual injury, sometimes serious, can be done to the plants.

KILLING POND WEEDS

There are times when water lilies become naturalized in ponds and grow so vigorously that they completely cover the water surface, becoming pests instead of ornamentals. Cattails and arrowheads also can become established in the border of a shallow pond, and quickly take over to such an extent that they become most objectionable. Sodium arsenite has been used to rid pools of these pests without injuring the fish.

The current brush killers (2,4-D plus 2,4,5-PT including Dowpon) have also proved successful, used at the same rates of dilution recommended for killing brush. These are lightly sprayed on the exposed above-water surfaces of the plant parts during the active growing season. It is most important to spray in the late spring or early summer when the plants are growing actively, for succulent, vigorous, growing leaves absorb the materials better and result in a better kill. Using the same material late in the summer may have few apparent results, but timely applications can eradicate many water plants that become pests.

Large ponds have been successfully sprayed by helicopter. Two pounds of acid equivalent, 2,4-D, and 2 pounds of acid equivalent 2,4,5-PT are used in a one gallon mixture, and this in turn was mixed with 2 gallons of water and sprayed from the helicopter at the rate of 3 gallons of this mixture per acre. When this spray was applied in early summer, excellent control of water lilies was obtained by October.

Small pools covered with algae (and without fish) can be "cleaned" with the use of potassium permanganate at 4 parts per million of water, or copper sulfate at the rate of 2 pounds per million gallons of water. Though this will certainly kill any fish in the pool, and may be strong enough to injure water lilies present, it has its value for pool cleaning.

However, before using any of these materials on ponds, especially those with outlets to streams, one should check with the local Pest Control Board to ascertain the restrictions against treating such pools with chemicals. Many boards have strict rules now as the result of the recent water pollution laws that have been enacted in many states.

LABOR-SAVING MACHINES

The individual desires of the gardener as well as his needs, true and fancied, will govern the types of garden machinery that are accumulated over the years. The man who enjoys gardening for the fun and exercise he gets out of it will have few gadgets—few unless he also happens to be afflicted with an inquisitive mechanical twist, in which event he may eventually buy them all. Of course, the size of the garden determines whether or not large expenditures should be made for complicated machinery that is used infrequently. New types and makes of machines appear every year, and one has only to read the ads in the major horticultural magazines to know what such machines are and where they can be obtained.

Any machine reduces hand labor, but the main criterion is whether it stays in working order long enough, without repair, to pay for its purchase price. Thereby hangs many a sad tale, but each individual has to cross this mechanical-obstacle bridge some time or other, and whether he buys more than he can use is not a problem we can deal with here. There are only a few things that can be said in this connection.

Lawn Mowers: The popular types now being used in the greatest numbers are those with horizontally revolving blades. These can be dangerous if safety measures are not taken, but they come in so many sizes and models that anything from grass to seedling trees and shrubs nearly an inch in diameter can be cut with them. They are also ideal for cutting low ground covers and can do the job at a higher level than the old-fashioned reel-type mowers. Another advantage is that keeping them sharpened for clean cutting is relatively simple, since all that is needed is a file, emery wheel, or grindstone. The reel type of mower, on the other hand, is comparatively difficult to sharpen and keep properly adjusted.

However, in buying a mower with a rotary type of blade one should be certain to obtain a machine that does not leave the cut grass in one small line or strip, but rather has enough power to blow the grass clippings and distribute them over a wide area. The reason for this is simple, but it is one I had to learn by firsthand experience.

When one owns a rotary-blade mower, the tendency is to let the grass grow taller and to mow less frequently. When the heavy clippings are deposited in a thin line by the mower, they may be so dense that they kill the living grass underneath. When this happens, bare spots quickly occur, followed by the intrusion of Crab Grass and other lawn weeds. Thus a beautiful lawn can be ruined in a few short weeks. This actually happened to ours, and the situation was augmented by the fact that the lawn was inadvertently fertilized (it really did not need fertilizer), thus making the grass clippings heavier. The use of a reel-type mower would have helped to spread the clippings evenly, as would some type of blowing mechanism with a rotary blade mower.

Labor can also be eliminated if the grass is not fertilized too much or too often. Some people like to maintain a perfect lawn of green grass, and in order to do so must fertilize, water, and cut frequently. There are many situations where such a lawn adds to the overall landscape picture, and the time and money spent in its maintenance are considered well spent. On the other hand, there are lawns not in this classification; there are areas where green grass is appropriate and necessary, but as long as it is green and not too tall, and as long as it does not die out in spots, it serves its purpose well. Such lawns need not be fertilized too frequently or cut too often. The rotary mowers are ideal for cutting these, since many of them can be adjusted to cut easily at higher levels than one would ordinarily use to cut with a reel-type mower. Lawn sweepers and riding sulkies are only a few of the mower "accessories" we are continually being urged to buy to make this one garden chore easier.

Speaking from experience, I have seen our large lawn in its ups and downs over the last twenty-five years. When our children were at home to mow it, it was sometimes cut too often, merely so an energetic youngster could earn a little extra spending money. As they grew older it became more and more of a chore, regardless of the cash reward at the end of the job. Now that I am left with it, and it takes all of two hours to cut, naturally I am experimenting with all sorts of heights at which it may be cut, and with machines as well, to see how long the grass can grow and then be cut without making raking a necessity. Needless to say, under this regime it has not been fertilized for many years, and when summer drought brings out dead spots it is merely a matter of interest to note how long it takes for grass to grow back in again once the rains come. It is not what many would call a perfect lawn, but it is green most of the time, and it is cut.

Leaf Shredders: The restrictions on burning in the open, now forced upon many communities in order to alleviate air pollution, bring up the problem of what to do with dead leaves in the fall. For years it has been recommended that these be placed in the compost heap to be used later for soil improvement. Now, many a homeowner is forced to do so. Many types of leaf shredders are available that are great aids in doing this work. One we bought was advertised as being able to reduce 20 bushels of dry leaves into one bushel—and it did just that. Instead of using all the shredded material on a compost pile, we put a two-inch layer of shredded leaves about the plants in the garden in the fall, at the time they were shredded. This mulch aided materially in bringing plants through the winter in better condition, and as they rotted during the following year, they greatly improved the soil. Shredded material left over from this operation was put in a compost pile at the back of the garden together with weeds and lawn clippings. This operation has greatly improved the growth of all our plants.

Brush Chippers: Some leaf shredders are powerful enough to chip brush as well as leaves. If there is need of much brush chipping each year, these larger machines might be considered. One should, however, carefully estimate the amount of brush he will have each year, as well as the size of the branches, to determine whether a large machine, that is pretty heavy and hard to move around and store, is going to be worth the expenditure.

Fertilizer Spreaders: If the lawn is to be fertilized, a simple, pushable, fertilizer spreader is a good investment. They are available with standard calibrations for most of the standard fertilizers.

Soil Cultivators: There are many garden gadgets for working the soil, both man-operated and machine-operated. Certainly the right machine can eliminate a great deal of hand labor. This is especially true with the mechanical rotary hoes. The larger the garden area that needs to be redug each year, the more important a machine becomes. It must be kept in mind that almost every community has such machines for hire, with or without operators. Years ago, when the suburban home-owner planned his vegetable garden, he would have to make arrangements with the nearest farmer to have the garden plowed by a team of horses. Today the rotary hoe takes their place and saves all the spading and digging and hoeing.

Other Garden Machines: The small, engine-operated dusters and sprayers available can deteriorate fast unless cared for properly. The same is true of fertilizer spreaders. Small chain saws do make work easy on the tree-covered suburban grounds, and many a gardener purchases one even though careful consideration would show him that he did not have enough work to justify the expense of buying one. Here again it might be cheaper to rent a machine or even have the work done; but chain saws, regardless of whether they are operated by electricity or gasoline engines, do make work easier and faster.

If one desires a careful edge kept on the perennial border, there are inexpensive gasoline or electrically operated edgers available. It takes a little practice to keep the edge straight with these machines, but once the task is mastered one can edge a border or walk using far less physical exertion than with the spade and hoe.

Clipping the hedge need not be so strenuous either. Electric shears are available, operated with the house current. These mechanically operated shears can be used on certain types of hedges that do not grow too vigorously. These tools are assets, and save the sore arms that result from a few hours' effort with the old-fashioned hedge shears. Better still, of course, would be to use hedge plants that grow only to a certain height. More will be said elsewhere about these most desirable plants (see pages 136–140).

Wheelbarrows or garden carts made of aluminum save extra exertion and should be bought wherever they can be used appropriately.

There is always a machine-minded addict who wants to sell himself a bill of goods. This is the man who finally invests in a combination tractor affair that will dig the garden and cultivate it, that will mow the grass and at the same time pull a riding sulky, that will plow the snow on walk or driveway (the advertisement never mentioned how much snow or how heavy), and that will also saw wood. Well, there are such machines, but the smaller they are, the less they will do all these things effectively. One should thoroughly understand his own needs, and then be certain the machine he is considering can do the job or jobs effectively, before he tries to short-cut some needed exercise by yielding to the machine age completely.

The individual who wants to reduce hand labor by the use of mechanical devices can have a field day deciding which machines to purchase. Ultimately a realization of his own ability (or inability) to do the work will dictate to him what form his purchases should take.

VACATIONING HOUSE PLANTS

All house plants are not amenable to being given a vacation outdoors unattended during the summer, but fortunate is the person who can select types that are. A shaded spot where the soil is good and does not dry out proves best. Where such a spot is not available, it may be impossible to place house plants outdoors, for the hot summer sun can quickly dry up or burn many tender plants.

Our situation is rather fortunate, for we have selected a cool spot near the house under a large and dense Canada Hemlock. Every other year we add generous amounts of manure to the soil, so that there is plenty of organic matter. The location is within reach of the hose so that it can easily be watered during droughts. Otherwise, the plants receive no attention.

They are set out as soon as all danger from frost is over; taken out of their pots, they are merely set in the soil and cut back, for usually some have grown long and lanky during the winter months indoors. Nothing much is done to them until about the first of September, when they are potted, but still left outdoors in the same place to become acclimated. Just before frost they are brought into the house—it's as simple as that.

It should be pointed out that experience and many trials have shown us the proper spot, and we have confined ourselves to growing types of plants that can be handled this way. Having given considerable care to house plants indoors for eight months of the year, we are ready for a vacation from these chores, and frequently the plants are ready for a vacation from our somewhat haphazard care! In any event this system works well, and is about the easiest possible arrangement that can be made for the "vacation" period of house plants. Some of the plants growing well under this nice arrangement are:

Aspidistra elatior	Aspidistra
Begonia semperflorens	Wax Begonia
Cacti species	Cacti
Chlorophytum elatum	Spider Plant
Cissus incisa	Grape-ivy Treebine
Crassula argentea	Jade Plant
Dracena species	Dracena
Fatshedera lizei	Fatshedera
Ferns—several genera and species	Ferns
Ficus elastica	Indian Rubber-plant
Hedera helix	English Ivy
Kalanchoe species	Kalanchoe

Peperomia obtusifolia	Oval-leaf Peperomia
Persea americana	Avocado
Philodendron species	Philodendron
Plectranthus oertendahlii	Swedish Ivy
Sansevieria species	Sansevieria
Saxifraga stolonifera	Mother-of-thousands
Tolmiaea menziesii	Piggy-back Plant
Zebrina pendula	Wandering Jew

3

Low Maintenance
Plant Lists

The plants in the following lists have been selected because of their low maintenance needs. Few have serious pests, although it will be admitted by everyone that certain plants may have local pests on occasion. The ones listed have not had serious pest troubles in our experience. It has been most disconcerting to eliminate some of the best of the ornamentals from the following lists (such as azaleas, euonymus, roses, and rhododendrons) merely because they may have had one or two serious pests or were overly particular concerning soil requirements. Their elimination merely points up the fact that they do require special care, and because of this have no place in this book on easy maintenance.

The hardiness zones given refer to the hardiness map on the inside book covers. This is the same map used by the author in *Wyman's Gardening Encyclopedia*. Most gardeners are accustomed to using this map by this time, and realize that when a plant is listed as hardy in Zone 4 it will usually be hardy in Zones 5 to 9; in other words, it can also be grown farther South until summer heat or drought, rather than winter cold, become the modifying factors. Also, it may be possible to grow the same plant in certain sheltered spots in colder regions. No zonal map of hardiness is complete, and many local variations in altitude or climate must be taken into consideration when selecting plants for any garden.

Time of bloom given is that for the vicinity of Boston, Massachusetts. The blooming period can be set ahead the farther south one goes.

Plants normally blooming together in Boston, Massachusetts; Rochester, New York; Detroit, Michigan; Chicago, Illinois; and Seattle, Washington; would bloom approximately so many weeks earlier in the following places:

New York, New York; Columbus, Ohio; Philadelphia, Pennsylvania; London, England	2 weeks
Washington, D.C.; Lexington, Kentucky; Asheville, North Carolina	3 weeks
St. Louis, Missouri	5 weeks
Augusta, Georgia	8 weeks

and in Portland, Maine, and southern Canada, they would bloom 1½ weeks *later*.

Available low maintenance plants are divided into the following lists in this chapter, for quick selection. All are listed alphabetically and described in Chapter 4, pages 197–358. It is well to keep these lists in mind when hunting for a plant to fulfill a particular need.

Obviously, the heights of plants are extremely important in making plans for a garden or landscape planting. In small gardens with low-foundation plantings, the shrubs under 3 feet high are the most important;

Number of Plants (or Groups) Listed

Bulbs	53
Perennials	106
Woody Vines	37
Ground Covers	87
Bank Plants	31
Labor-saving Hedge Plants Under 6 Feet Tall	60
Low Woody Plants for Accent in the Perennial Garden	41
Dual-purpose Plants	30
Plants for Dry Soils	49
Plants for Wet Soils	34
Plants for Shade	110
Plants for City Gardens	65
Shrubs—Flowering and Fruiting	81
Trees—Flowering and Fruiting	38
Trees and Shrubs with Colored Foliage	59
Plants Creating Work	54

you will seldom need any that are over 4 to 5 feet high —just under eye level is best. The larger the garden, of course, the larger the shrubs that are needed to afford the correct landscape proportions.

Especially valuable to owners of small one-story homes are the small trees under 35 feet at maturity, the newer trees that are proving popular in modern plantings. Some of the larger trees are also given, but it is the smaller ones that are meeting favor on every side, for they are often less exepnsive, and are easier and cheaper to care for. They do not grow out of scale, and if they must eventually be removed for one purpose or another, the removal costs are lower.

Selecting low plants for the low house is extremely important. The reader is urged to go through the alphabetical list (pages 197–358) carefully when he is seeking a plant to serve at a definite height. The various size groups and number of plants in each group as are follows:

Shrubs under 1½ feet	70
Shrubs 1½–3 feet	66
Shrubs 4–5 feet	68
Shrubs 6–9 feet	141
Shrubs 10–15 feet	62
Shrubs 15 feet and over	40
Trees 20–35 feet	77
Trees over 35 feet	178

The author offers the plant lists on the following pages as a helpful method of making quick selections of good, low maintenance plants for specific purposes. He realizes that there may be insect or disease pests attacking some of these plants in local areas, and that those experienced in horticulture will know of other low maintenance plants that might be listed either on a local or on a national scale. However, offering such lists —even though full agreement may never be reached concerning them—will aid independent thinking and experimentation on the subject, which is certainly all to the good.

Letters given at the left hand side of the scientific names of these plants in the following lists and in the A to Z listing (Chapter 4, pages 197–358) are provided for quick identification of plant properties:

E—Woody plant with evergreen foliage

E-D or D-E—Woody plant that is either deciduous or evergreen, depending on location

H—Herbaceous plant, the foliage dies to the ground in winter

B—Bulbs or bulblike plants
   (If no E, H, or B is given, the plant is a deciduous woody plant.)

x—Placed before a plant name means the plant is of hybrid origin.

' '—Single quotes—as 'Barbara Ann'—indicate that

the plant is a clone or cultivar which will not breed true from seed, but must be asexually propagated by cutting, budding, or grafting.

Time of Bloom given (between the Flower Color and the Hardiness Zone) is for the approximate time the plant blooms in the vicinity of Boston, Massachusetts. (See page 100 for approximate time of bloom in other areas.)

LOW MAINTENANCE BULBS AND BULBLIKE PLANTS

Every garden needs its full complement of bulbs in the flower borders, in the foundation plantings about the house, or naturalized in the open where they will be conspicuous when they bloom in the spring.

The soil should be well prepared to a depth of at least 6 inches (and sometimes deeper in the case of large bulbs). If they are to be interplanted among shrubs or perennials, dig a hole and remove all the poor soil. Mix in advance some good soil with a little decayed leaf mold and fertilizer. Sometimes bone meal is suggested. This mixture can be carried around in a bucket if only a few bulbs are to be planted in each spot. Place some of this good soil mixture at the bottom of the hole, then place the bulb on top of this mixture at the proper depth and fill in with the same good mixture.

The depth of planting, in general, is about two and a half times the width of the bulb. This means that the bottom of some of the larger bulbs is 6 inches or more under the soil surface.

The time to plant most bulbs is in the fall, usually by mid-October, but there are exceptions. In the list that follows, the Summer-hyacinth (*Galtonia candicans*) and the Tiger-flower (*Tigridia pavonia*) might best be planted in the spring. Late summer is the best time to plant some of the fall blooming crocuses and the Common Autumn-crocus (*Colchicum autumnale*) as well as the Autumn-amaryllis (*Lycoris squamigera*).

When planting is completed it is well to apply a good mulch (see Mulching, pp. 57–78) for this helps to protect the bulbs during the winter and prevents some of the more shallow-planted types from being pushed out of the soil by the alternate freezing and thawing of the ground during the colder months. It may be that in some areas rodents will eat a few of certain species, but this is one of the minor hazards that one will have to put up with.

Plant well, in good soil, at the proper time and right depths, mulch well, and then forget them. It is remarkable how bulbs will continue to surprise you each year with their bright blossoms—and minimum care.

LOW MAINTENANCE BULBS

SCIENTIFIC NAME	HEIGHT	FLOWER COLOR	TIME OF BLOOM	HARDI-NESS ZONE *	COMMON NAME
Allium albopilosum	3'	lilac	May	4	Stars-of-Persia
Allium flavum	2'	yellow	August	2–3	Yellow Onion
Allium giganteum	4'	blue	June	5	Giant Onion
Allium moly	1½'	yellow	June	2–3	Golden Garlic
Allium senescens glaucum	4–8"	pink	July	3	
Arisaema triphyllum	12–18"	green	June	4	Jack-in-the-pulpit
Bulbocodium vernum	6"	rose	April	5	Spring Meadow Saffron
Camassia cusickii	3'	blue	May	5	Cusick Camas
Camassia leichtinii	2'	blue	April	5	Leichtlin Camas
Chionodoxa luciliae	3"	white, blue	April	4	Glory-of-the-snow
Colchicum autumnale	6"	purple	October	4	Common Autumn-crocus or Meadow Saffron

* Remember, you can grow most of the plants listed for zones *colder* than yours.

LOW MAINTENANCE BULBS (continued)

SCIENTIFIC NAME	HEIGHT	FLOWER COLOR	TIME OF BLOOM	HARDI-NESS ZONE *	COMMON NAME
Convallaria majalis	8"	white	May	2–3	Lily-of-the-valley
Crocus sativus	3–6"	white	fall	6	Saffron Crocus
Crocus speciosus	3–6"	blue	September	5	
Crocus susianus	3–6"	yellow	March	4	Cloth-of-gold Crocus
Crocus vernus	3–6"	white, blue	March	4	Common Crocus
Crocus zonatus	3–6"	rose	fall	5	
Eranthis hyemalis	3"	yellow	April	4	Winter Aconite
Erythronium ameri-canum	1'	yellow	March	3	Common Fawn-lily
Erythronium dens-canis	6"	rose	March	2–3	Dogtooth Fawn-lily
Erythronium grandi-florum	2'	yellow	March	5	Lamb's Tongue Fawn-lily

* Remember, you can grow most of the plants listed for zones *colder* than yours.

Fritillaria meleagris	1'	red, yellow	April	3	Guinea-hen Flower
Galanthus elwesii	1'	white	March	4	Giant Snowdrop
Galanthus nivalis	8"	white	March	3	Snowdrop
Galtonia candicans	3–4'	white	August	5	Summer-hyacinth
Hyacinthus orientalis	15"	white, red, blue, yellow	April	6	Common Hyacinth
Lilium amabile	3–4'	red	June	2–3	Korean Lily
Lilium auratum	3–12'	white, red	August–September	4	Goldband Lily
Lilium canadense	2–5'	yellow, red	July	3	Canada Lily
Lilium candidum	3½'	white	June	4	Madonna Lily
Lilium pumilum	1½'	red	June	3	Coral Lily
Lilium regale	4–6'	white	July	3	Regal Lily
Lilium speciocum	4–5'	red, white	August	4	Speciosum Lily
Lilium superbum	6–10'	orange	July–August	5	Turkscap Lily
Lilium tigrinum	3–4'	red	July	3	Tiger Lily

LOW MAINTENANCE BULBS (continued)

SCIENTIFIC NAME	HEIGHT	FLOWER COLOR	TIME OF BLOOM	HARDI-NESS ZONE *	COMMON NAME
Liriope spicata	8–12"	white	July–August	4	Creeping Lily-turf
Lycoris squamigera	2'	lilac	August–September	5	Autumn-amaryllis
Muscari armeniacum	1'	blue	May	4	Armenian Grape-hyacinth
Narcissus asturiensis	3–5"	yellow	April	4	Asturian Daffodil
Narcisssus bulbocodium	15"	yellow	April	6	Petticoat Daffodil
Narcissus cyclamineus	8"	yellow	April	6	Cyclamen Daffodil
Narcissus incomparabilis	1'	yellow	April	4	Nonesuch Daffodil

* Remember, you can grow most of the plants listed for zones *colder* than yours.

Narcissus jonquilla	1½'	yellow	April	4	Jonquil
Narcissus odorus	1'	yellow	April	6	Campernelle Jonquil
Narcissus poeticus	1½'	white	April	4	Poet's Narcissus
Narcissus pseudo-narcissus	15"	yellow	April	4	Daffodil
Narcissus tazetta	1½'	yellow	April	8	Polyanthus Narcissus
Narcissus triandrus	1'	white	April	4	Angels-tears
Ornithogalum umbellatum	1'	white	May–June	4	Star-of-Bethlehem
Scilla hispanica	20"	blue	April	4	Spanish Squill
Scilla sibirica	6"	blue	March	2–3	Siberian Squill
Tigridia pavonia	1½'	yellow-purple	summer	6	Tiger-flower, Mexican Shell-flower
Trillium grandiflorum	12–14"	white	April–June	4	Snow Trillium

LOW MAINTENANCE PERENNIALS

There are many perennials being grown in America today and the following list of 106 low maintenance plants includes only a small portion of the whole. Missing are many valued garden perennials like Delphinium, Sweet William (actually biennials), Shasta Daisy, Columbine hybrids and the like, with which we have struggled and given up for one reason or another. Possibly our problems were entirely local.

Most perennials can be transplanted either in the spring (before they start to grow) or in the fall. Give them good soil and a mulch (see Mulching, pages 57–78)—especially if fall transplanted—to keep the alternate freezing and thawing of the soil from actually pushing them out of the soil. Water well after transplanting and during summer droughts. The perennials listed are those we have found to be satisfactory during the past fifteen years. Throughout this period our perennials have all been growing in one garden, regularly mulched each fall and fertilized each spring. Many of the same plants we started with 15 years ago are still flourishing—ample proof that these are not fickle types, producing good flowers one year and disappearing the next. It will be noted also that these provide a colorful display of bloom from earliest spring until frost.

None have had serious insect or disease problems, in our experience, hence spraying for pest control is not practiced. When frost kills the above-ground parts, however, the entire garden is quickly scythed and raked clean. This kind of sanitary culture takes little time and may prevent considerable trouble the following year.

The following perennials can make a beautiful garden by themselves. The list can be expanded after one has personally experimented with other plants under local conditions.

110

PERENNIALS

SCIENTIFIC NAME	HEIGHT	COLOR OF FLOWER	TIME OF BLOOM	HARDI- NESS ZONE *	COMMON NAME
Achillea millefolium Rosea	6"–2'	pink	July–September	2	Pink Yarrow
Achillea ptarmica	2'	white	July–August	2–3	Sneezewort
Ajuga genevensis	6–9"	blue	May–June	2–3	Geneva Bugle
Ajuga reptans	4–12"	blue, purple	May–June	2–3	Bugleweed, Carpet Bugle
Ajuga reptans 'Variegata'	4–12"	white	May–June	2–3	White Carpet Bugle
Alyssum saxatile (See *Aurinia saxatilis*)					
Anchusa azurea	3–5'	blue	June–July	3	Italian Alkane, Italian Bugloss

* Remember, you can grow most of the plants listed for zones *colder* than yours.

PERENNIALS (continued)

SCIENTIFIC NAME	HEIGHT	COLOR OF FLOWER	TIME OF BLOOM	HARDI-NESS ZONE *	COMMON NAME
Anthemis tinctoria	3'	yellow	July–August	3	Golden Marguerite
Aquilegia canadensis	3'	yellow, red	July–August	2–3	American Columbine
Arabis albida 'Flore-pleno'	6–10"	white, pink	April–May	3	Double Wall Rock-cress
Arabis caucasica	4–10"	white	April–May	6	Caucasian Rock-cress
Artemisia lactiflora	4–5'	white	August–October	3	White Mugwort
Artemisia schmidtiana 'Nana'	4"	white	August–October	2–3	Silvermound Artemisia
Asclepias tuberosa	3'	orange	August–September	3	Butterfly Milkweed

* Remember, you can grow most of the plants listed for zones *colder* than yours.

Botanical name	Height	Color	Bloom time	Zone	Common name
Asperula odorata	8"	white	May–June	4	Sweet Woodruff
Aster frikartii 'Wonder of Staffa'	1½–2'	white, purple	July–November	4	
Aster novae-angliae	3–5'	pink	August	2–3	New England Aster
Aster novi-belgii	3–5'	white, purple	September–October	2–3	New York Aster
Astilbe japonica varieties	2'	white, red	June	5	Japanese Astilbe
Aurinia saxatilis	6"	yellow	April–May	3	Golden-tuft
Baptisia australis	3–4'	blue	May–June	2–3	Blue Wild Indigo
Caltha palustris	1–3'	yellow	April	3	Marsh Marigold
Campanula carpatica	1'	blue	July	3	Carpathian Bellflower
Campanula latifolia	3'	blue	July	3	Great Bellflower
Campanula percisifolia	3'	blue, white	July–August	3	Peach-leaved Bellflower
Centaurea dealbata	2'	red, white	June–September	3	Persian Centaurea

113

PERENNIALS (continued)

SCIENTIFIC NAME	HEIGHT	COLOR OF FLOWER	TIME OF BLOOM	HARDI-NESS ZONE *	COMMON NAME
Centaurea montana	2'	blue	May–July	2–3	Mountain Bluet
Cerastium tomento-sum	3–6"	white	June	2–3	Snow-in-summer
Cheleone lyonii	3'	pink, purple	July–August	3	Pink Turtle-head
Cimicifuga racemosa	6–8'	white	June–September	2–3	Snakeroot, Cohash Bugbane
Coreopsis auriculata 'Nana'	6"	yellow	June–August	4	Dwarf Eared Coreopsis
Coreopsis verticillata	2½'	yellow	July–August	6	Threadleaf Coreopsis

* Remember, you can grow most of the plants listed for zones *colder* than yours.

Scientific Name	Height	Color	Bloom Time	Zone	Common Name
Coreopsis lanceolata	2'	yellow	July–August	3	Lance Coreopsis
Dianthus plumarius	1½'	pink, white	May–June	3	Grass Pink, Cottage Pink
Dianthus gratianopolitanus	4"	pink	July	3	Cheddar Pink
Dicentra eximia	1–2'	pink	May–September	2–3	Fringed Bleeding-heart
Dicentra formosa	1'	pink	May–September	2–3	Pacific Bleeding-heart
Dicentra spectabilis	2'	pink	May–June	2–3	Common Bleeding-heart
Dictamnus albus	3'	white, purple	July	2–3	Gasplant
Doronicum causasicum	2'	yellow	May–June	4	Caucasian Leopardsbane
Echinacea purpurea	3½'	red, purple	July–August	3	Purple Echinacea
Echinops exaltatus	3–12'	blue	July–September	3	Russian Globe-thistle
Echinops ritro	1–2'	blue	July–September	3	Small Globe-thistle

PERENNIALS (continued)

SCIENTIFIC NAME	HEIGHT	COLOR OF FLOWER	TIME OF BLOOM	HARDI-NESS ZONE *	COMMON NAME
Epimedium alpinum rubrum	6–9″	red, yellow	May–June	3	Red Alpine Epimedium
Epimedium grandi-florum	9″	red, yellow	May–June	3	Long-spur Epimedium, Bishop's-hat
Epimedium pinnatum	9–12″	yellow	April–July	5	Persian Epimedium
Euphoibia epithy-moides	1′	yellow	summer	4	Cushion Euphorbia
Eupatorium macu-latum	6–10′	purple	August	2–3	Joe-pye-weed
Filipendula-ulmaria variegata	6′	white	June–July	2–3	Variegated Queen-of-the-meadow

* Remember, you can grow most of the plants listed for zones *colder* than yours.

Gaillardia aristata	2–3'	yellow, red	July–August
Geranium sanguineum	12"	red	May–August
Geranium sanguineum 'Prostratum'	6"	red	May–August
Gypsophila paniculata 'Bristol Fairy'	3'	white	July
Gypsophila repens 'Rosea'	18"	pink	June–August
Helenium autumnale	6'	yellow	July–August
Helianthus tuberosus	12'	yellow	August–September
Hemerocallis flava	3'	yellow	June
Hemerocallis fulva	2½–3'	orange, red	July–August

2–3	Common Blanket-flower	
3	Blood-red Geranium	
3	Dwarf Blood-red Geranium	
2–3	Double Baby's-breath	
3	Rosy Creeping Gypsophila	
3	Common Sneezeweed	
4	Jerusalem Artichoke	
3	Lemon Daylily	
2–3	Tawny Daylily	

PERENNIALS (continued)

SCIENTIFIC NAME	HEIGHT	COLOR OF FLOWER	TIME OF BLOOM	HARDI- NESS ZONE *	COMMON NAME
Heuchera sanguinea	1–2′	red	May–September	3	Coral-bells
Hosta decorata	1–2′	blue	July	3	Blunt Plantain-lily
Hosta fortunei	2′	lavender	July	3	Fortune's Plantain-lily
Hosta lancifolia 'Albo- marginata'	1½–2′	lavender	August	3	Variegated Narrow- leaved Plantain-lily
Hosta plantaginea	10″	white	August	3	Fragrant Plantain-lily
Hosta sieboldiana	18″	lilac	July	3	Siebold Plantain-lily
Hosta undulata	2–3′	lavender	July	3	Wavy-leaved Plantain- lily
Iberis sempervirens	12″	white	April–May	3	Evergreen Candytuft
Iris kaempferi	2′	white, red, blue	June–July	4	Japanese Iris

* Remember, you can grow most of the plants listed for zones *colder* than yours.